Hans-Günter Heumann

Piano Junior

A Creative and Interactive
Piano Course for Children

Lesson Book 3

ED 13803

Illustrations by Leopé

SCHOTT

Mainz · London · Berlin · Madrid · New York · Paris · Prague · Tokyo · Toronto
© 2017 SCHOTT MUSIC Ltd. London. Printed in Germany

About the Author

Hans-Günter Heumann is a freelance composer and author, living in southern Germany.

Since studying piano, composition, and music pedagogy at the Musikhochschule Hannover, followed by further studies in the USA, he has dedicated himself to the editing of pedagogical piano material. He has a particular interest in presenting music in an accessible way to reach a broad audience.

Based on many years of experience teaching children, young people and adults, Hans-Günter has written a great number of internationally successful and award winning publications, and has composed and arranged piano music in a range of styles for beginners to advanced students.

Having developed successful, methodical concepts for learning how to play the piano for all age groups and abilities, Hans-Günter's work has been translated into many different languages and sold millions of copies, an indication of the wide-spread appreciation of his work.
His publications *Klavierspielen – mein schönstes Hobby* and *Piano Kids* (both published by Schott Music) have become two of the most significant piano methods in the German language.

Acknowledgments

The author and publishers would like to thank Prof. Carolyn True, Melanie Spanswick and Dr. Sally Cathcart for expert suggestions, support and advice in the development of *Piano Junior*.

ED 13803
British Library Cataloguing-in-Publication Data.
A catalogue record for this book is available from the British Library
ISMN 979-0-2201-3639-9
ISBN 978-1-84761-427-8

© 2017 Schott Music Ltd, London

All rights reserved. No part of this publication may be reproduced,
stored in a retrieval system, or transmitted, in any form or by any
means, electronic, mechanical, photocopying, recording or otherwise,
without prior written permission from Schott Music Ltd,
48 Great Marlborough Street, London W1F 7BB

English translation: Schott London Editorial
Design by Barbara Brümmer
Typesetting Barbara Brümmer
Music setting: Darius-Heise-Krzyszton
Stockphotos: Icons (Playing Corner, Composing Corner)
Cover design: www.adamhaystudio.com
Audio tracks recorded, mixed and mastered by Clements Pianos
Audio tracks performed by Samantha Ward and Maciej Raginia
Printed in Germany S&Co. 9201

Introduction

Piano Junior is a creative and interactive piano course for children from the age of 6, which progresses in small, manageable steps. It is a fun and satisfying approach to playing and learning about music, encouraging quick and noticeable progress.

Piano Junior is home to PJ, a robot with great enthusiasm for the piano, who accompanies and motivates children throughout the piano course. On PJ's homepage **www.piano-junior.com** you will find audio tracks of all pieces played on an acoustic piano, further fun practise resources and other interactive elements.

This innovative course stimulates and encourages creativity through regular, integrated 'Corners', such as *Composing, Improvising, Action, Playing, Technique, Ear Training, Memory, Sight-Reading* and *Music Quizzes*. In this way solid musical knowledge and technical ability is acquired. The experience of learning the piano is multifaceted: aural – with regular ear-training exercises; visual – with sight-reading; tactile – with clear explanations of technical aspects of playing and, above all, creative – with exercises in composing and improvising.

The choice of pieces includes attractive pieces from the classical period to the present day as well as interesting arrangements of folk tunes and children's songs, classical masterpieces, jazz and pop melodies.

In addition to the **Lesson Book** (which includes Exercises) at each level there is also: a **Theory Book**, in which valuable information from the method is worked through and consolidated in a playful, imaginative way. There is also a **Duet Book** at each level, to provide motivation for playing the piano with others and a **Performance Book** with great repertoire, which is fun to play. The *Flash Cards* included can be used to provide further practice in note reading, with musical symbols/terms and with rhythm patterns. By collecting the cards from each volume you will acquire a wealth of reference material.

Music greatly enriches the life of a child and **Piano Junior** aims to provide a musical basis for this in the most creative and motivating way.

Hans-Günter Heumann

Reference to:		References to material at **www.piano-junior.com**:	
Theory Book		▶ Audio Track **1** | Rhythm Check **1** | Workout **1** | Sight-Reading **1**	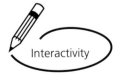 Interactivity
Duet Book			
Performance Book			

Contents

Summary of Book 2	6
Welcome Piece: **Ode to Joy** Metronome	8
UNIT 1: Extending the Hand Position	10
Exercises Changing fingers on the same key	10
Twinkle, Twinkle, Little Star	11
The Moon has Risen	12
The Moon has Risen, Variations	13
Spreading Your Fingers **Exercises**	14
Michael, Row the Boat Ashore	15
Brother John	16
Brother John, Canon	17
UNIT 2: Interval of a Sixth	18
Oh, Susanna	18
Boogie-Woogie Stomp	20
Funny PJ Dance con moto	22
UNIT 3: Extending the Range of Notes in RH	24
Minuetto	24
Sonatina	26
UNIT 4: Walking Fingers	28
Exercise	28
Autumn Leaves espressivo, Sequence	30
UNIT 5: Interval of a Seventh	32
Cool Junior Jazz	32
UNIT 6: Interval of an Octave	34
Octave Polka	34
UNIT 7: Passing Under	36
Exercise	36
Crossing Over	37
Exercise	37
Tightrope Dancer grazioso	38
Little Melodic Exercise Opus	39
My Bonnie Lies Over the Ocean	40
UNIT 8: Major Scales	42
C Major Scale Exercises	44
The Scale non troppo	45
Piano Halfpipe	46
UNIT 9: Playing Triads	48

C Major Triad/Chord	48
C Major Triad Exercise	49
UNIT 10: Primary Triads I IV V	50
Primary Triads in C Major	50
Primary Triads Exercise	50
Hula Hoop vivo	51
UNIT 11: Primary Triads and Inversions	52
Primary Triads with Inversions in C Major	52
Aloha	53
On Top of Old Smoky	54
On Top of Old Smoky, Variation	55
UNIT 12: Dominant Seventh Chord V7	56
Preliminary Exercise	56
Down in the Lowlands	57
Cancan simile	58
UNIT 13: Minor Scales	60
Natural A Minor Scale	60
Whitewater Rafting	61
Sad and Happy Amadeus	62
Harmonic A Minor Scale	64
Melodic A Minor Scale	64
Flying Carpet	65
UNIT 14: Primary Triads I IV V7	66
Primary Triads in A Minor	66
Primary Triads with Inversions in A Minor	66
Preliminary Exercise	67
Bella ciao	67
UNIT 15: The Right Pedal (Sustaining Pedal)	68
Moonlight	69
What Shall We Do with the Drunken Sailor	70
Daily Finger Fitness 3	72
Important Words and Signs	86
Certificate of Merit	88

Flash Cards 3 (inserts):
Notes, Musical Symbols/Terms, Rhythm

Summary of Book 2

Intervals

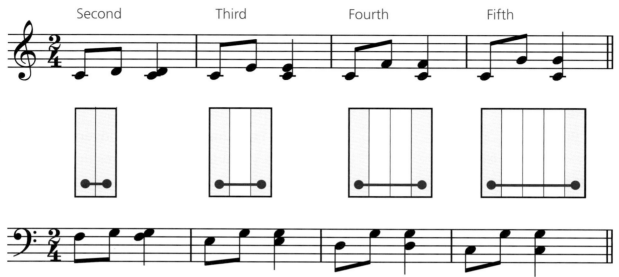

Second   Third   Fourth   Fifth

Notes and Rests

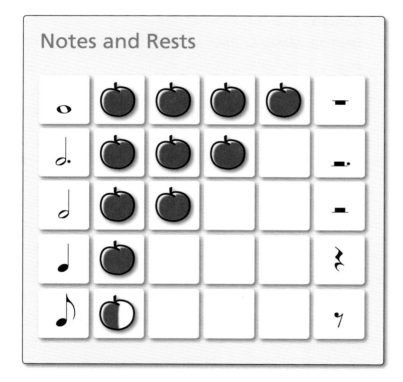

Rhythm Pyramid

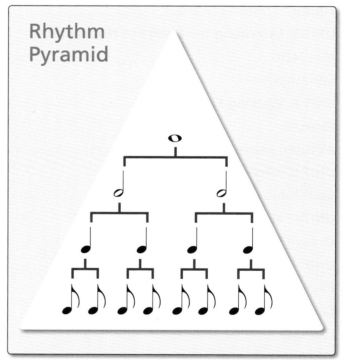

Dotted Crotchet / Quarter Note

Musical Terms

C = 4/4

- **marcato**
- **poco a poco**
- **dolce**
- **maestoso**

- **rit. / ritard.**
- **dim. / dimin.**
- **cresc.**
- **decresc.**

- **Adagio**
- **Allegretto**
- **Presto**

- **A-B-A**
- #
- ♭
- ♮

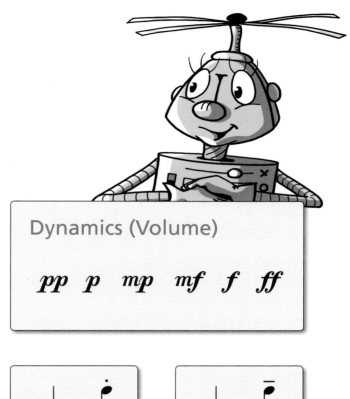

Dynamics (Volume)

pp *p* *mp* *mf* *f* *ff*

Range of Book 2

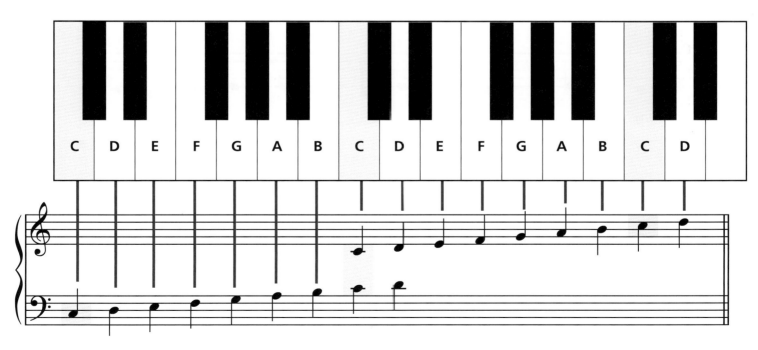

C D E F G A B C D E F G A B C D

7

Welcome Piece

Welcome to PIANO JUNIOR level 3! Let's start with a very famous melody from *Symphony No. 9* by Ludwig van Beethoven.

Ode to Joy

from Symphony No. 9

 page 72, No. 1–2

Ludwig van Beethoven (1770–1827)
Arr.: HGH

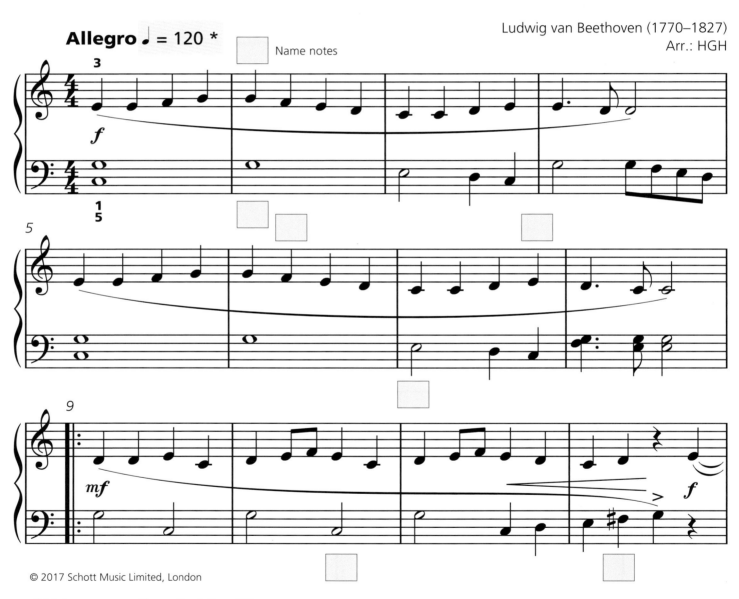

© 2017 Schott Music Limited, London

*) **Metronome**, see Theory Book 3, p. 6/7

 Ludwig van Beethoven was one of the greatest composers of classical music ever and a pupil of Joseph Haydn. His virtuoso piano playing and skill as a composer attracted numerous patrons who provided him with financial support. Despite increasing deafness, he still composed great masterpieces. Some famous pieces: *Für Elise, Moonlight Sonata, Symphony No. 5, Symphony No. 9 (Ode to Joy)*.

▶ Audio Track **1** | Rhythm Check **1**

1. Circle all the harmonic intervals in the LH.
2. Circle three examples of this rhythmic pattern:
3. Trace an accent and a cresc. sign.
4. Circle a sharp sign.

UNIT 1: Extending the Hand Position

Changing fingers on the same key

Exercises

Start this exercise using 2nd finger on RH and LH.

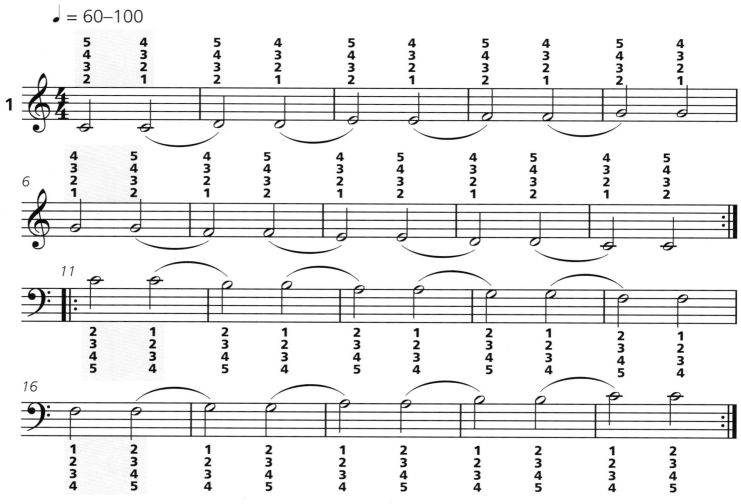

Start this exercise using 1st finger on RH and LH.

© 2017 Schott Music Limited, London

 **Finger Fitness** page 73/74, No. 3–4 **D3** page 4/5 **P3** page 4/5

Twinkle, Twinkle, Little Star

French Tune, 1761
Lyrics by Jane Taylor (1783–1824)
Arr.: HGH

Moderato ♩ = 116

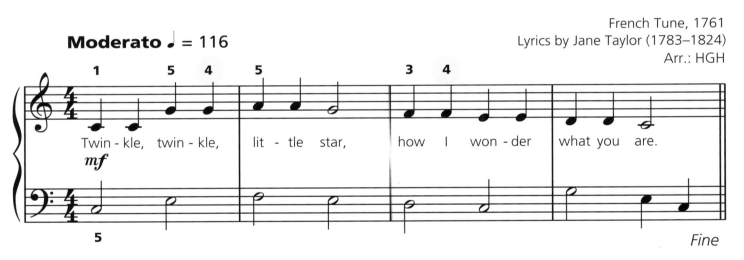

Twin - kle, twin - kle, lit - tle star, how I won - der what you are.

mf

Fine

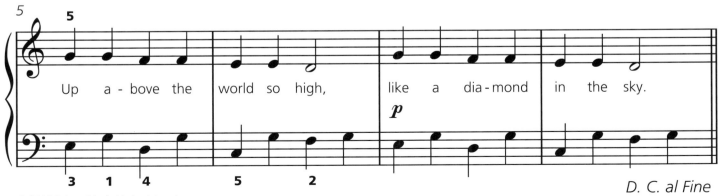

Up a - bove the world so high, like a dia - mond in the sky.

p

D. C. al Fine

© 2017 Schott Music Limited, London

 Finger Fitness page 74/75, No. 5–6 **T3** page 8/9 **P3** page 6

The Moon has Risen

German Folk Song
Arr.: HGH

Andante ♩ = 88

Name notes

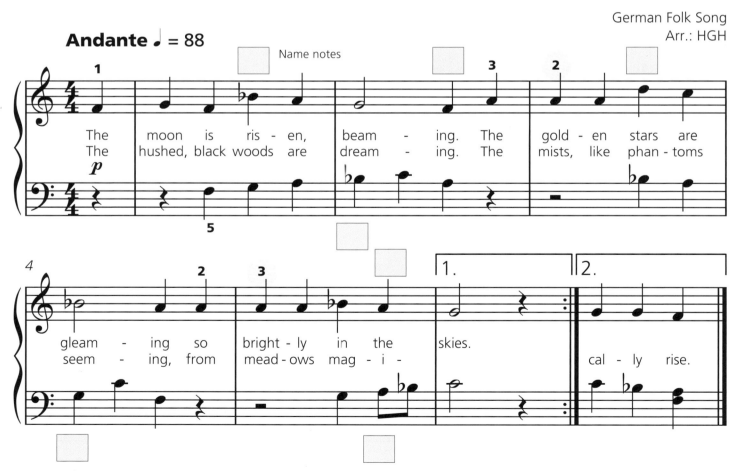

The moon is ris - en, beam - ing. The gold - en stars are
The hushed, black woods are dream - ing. The mists, like phan - toms

gleam - ing so bright - ly in the skies.
seem - ing, from mead - ows mag - i - cal - ly rise.

© 2017 Schott Music Limited, London

COMPOSING CORNER

Try playing THE MOON HAS RISEN in 3/4 time, too (see example 1) and with the rhythmic variation indicated in RH (see example 2). The first few bars/measures are shown here; you'll find it easy to play the rest. Aim to play all pieces from memory.
Try – especially with melodic pieces – to play the melody slightly louder than the accompaniment.

The Moon has Risen

Variations

Finger Fitness — page 75, No. 7

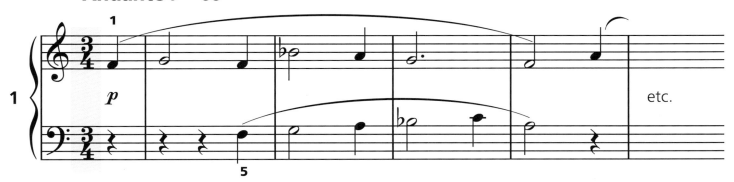

Rhythmic variation of the melody

© 2017 Schott Music Limited, London

Spreading Your Fingers
Exercises

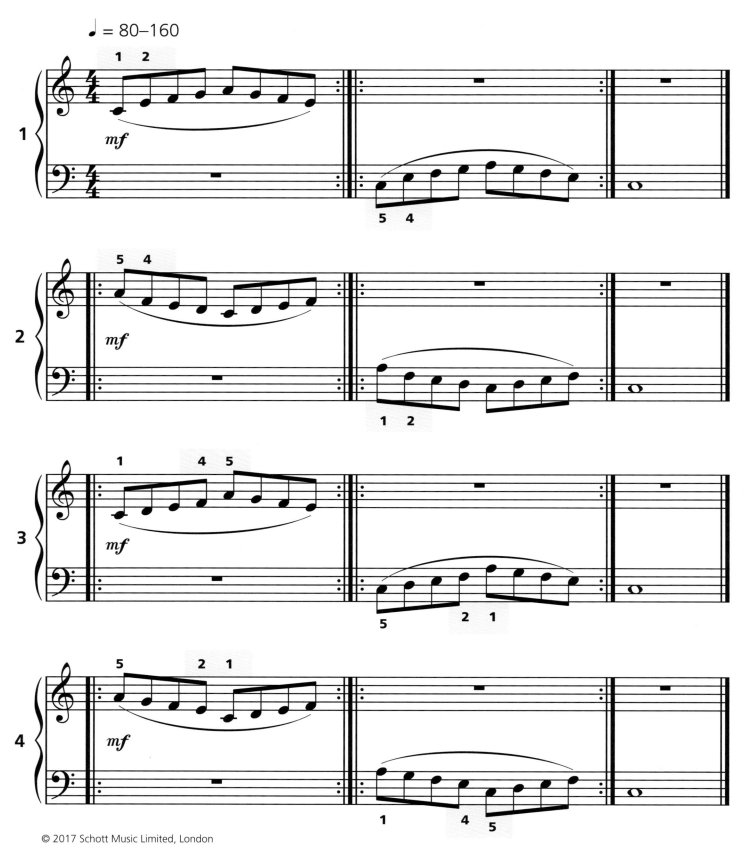

© 2017 Schott Music Limited, London

14

Michael, Row the Boat Ashore

♩ = 144

Spiritual
Arr.: HGH

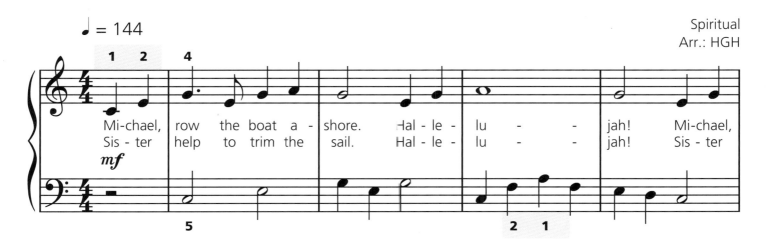

Mi-chael, row the boat a - shore. Hal - le - lu - - jah! Mi-chael,
Sis - ter help to trim the sail. Hal - le - lu - - jah! Sis - ter

mf

row the boat a - shore. Hal - le - lu - - - jah!
help to trim the sail. Hal - le - lu - - - jah!

© 2017 Schott Music Limited, London

Brother John

D3 page 8/9   **P3** page 8/9

♩ = 108

French Children's Song
Arr.: HGH

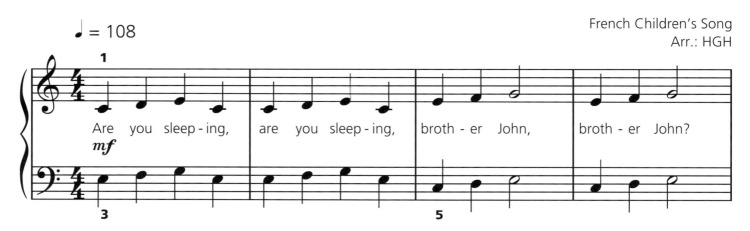

Are you sleep - ing, are you sleep - ing, broth - er John, broth - er John?

mf

Morn-ing bells are ring - ing, morn-ing bells are ring - ing: Ding, dang, dong, ding, dang, dong.

© 2017 Schott Music Limited, London

16

PLAYING CORNER

Play this piece starting on C and on G, too.

Canon

A **canon** is a polyphonic piece for several voices where all voices play or sing the same tune, one after another.

Brother John

Finger Fitness page 76, No.9

Canon

Circle the bar in which the first voice ends.

♩ = 108

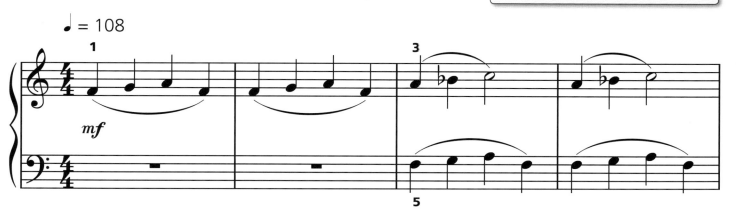

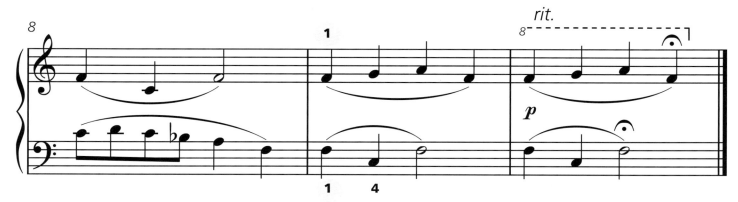

© 2017 Schott Music Limited, London

Unit 2: Interval of a Sixth

T3
page 12/13

On the piano

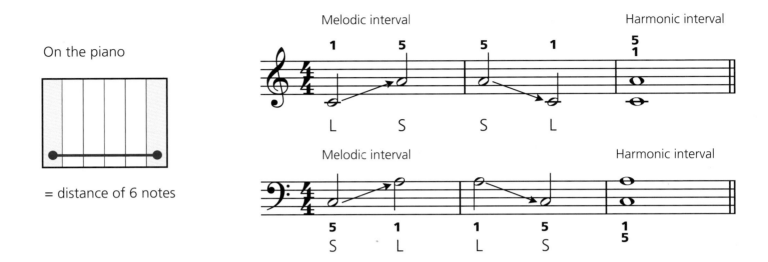

= distance of 6 notes

Oh, Susanna

Finger Fitness   page 76, No.10

D3 page 10/11   P3 page 10

♩ = 160

Stephen Collins Foster (1826–1864)
Arr.: HGH

come from A - la - ba - ma with a ban - jo on my knee, I'm___

© 2017 Schott Music Limited, London

▶ Video 3 | Audio Track 13 | Sight-Reading 4/5

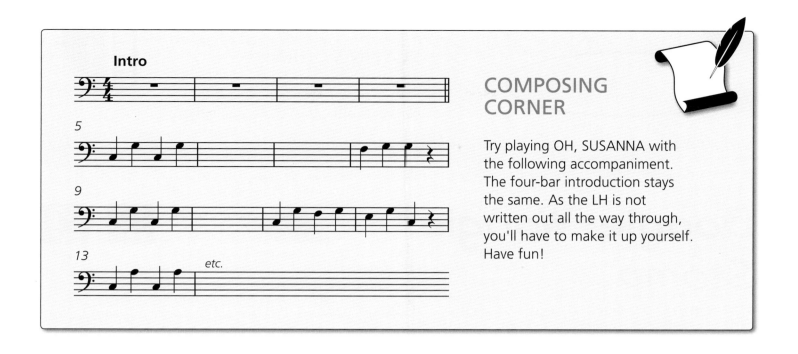

Intro

COMPOSING CORNER

Try playing OH, SUSANNA with the following accompaniment. The four-bar introduction stays the same. As the LH is not written out all the way through, you'll have to make it up yourself. Have fun!

going to Loui - si - a - na, my_____ true love for to see.

Oh, Su - san - na, oh, don't you cry for me, for I

come from A - la - ba - ma with a ban - jo on my knee.

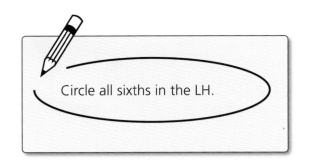

Circle all sixths in the LH.

PLAYING CORNER

Practise sections you find difficult to
play more often than those you find easier.

Boogie-Woogie* Stomp

Finger
Fitness   page 76/77,
No. 11–12   T3 page 14   P3 page 11

HGH

♩ = 132

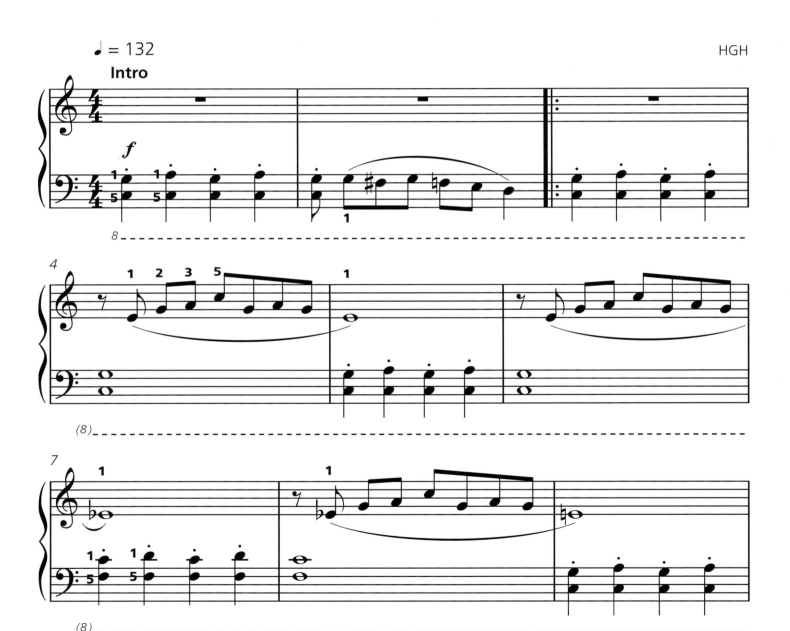

© 2017 Schott Music Limited, London

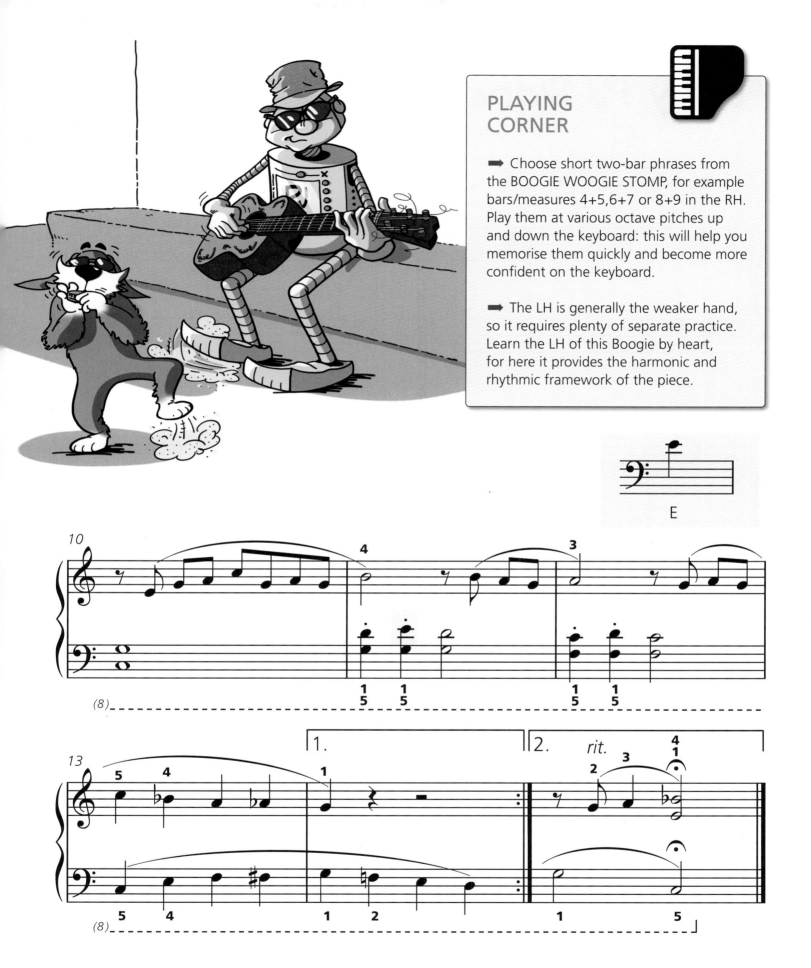

PLAYING CORNER

➡ Choose short two-bar phrases from the BOOGIE WOOGIE STOMP, for example bars/measures 4+5,6+7 or 8+9 in the RH. Play them at various octave pitches up and down the keyboard: this will help you memorise them quickly and become more confident on the keyboard.

➡ The LH is generally the weaker hand, so it requires plenty of separate practice. Learn the LH of this Boogie by heart, for here it provides the harmonic and rhythmic framework of the piece.

*) **Boogie-Woogie** is a blues piano style that emerged in abcut 1920 among African-Americans in Chicago. Typical of the boogie (-woogie) is a rigid bass pattern that stays the same all the time beneath a rhythmically varied melody.

Funny PJ Dance

Finger Fitness  page 78, No. 13-14 T3 page 15 P3 page 12/13

HGH

Con moto ♩ = 176

Name notes

© 2017 Schott Music Limited, London

▶ Audio Track **15** | Rhythm Check **6** | Workout **3** | Sight-Reading **7**

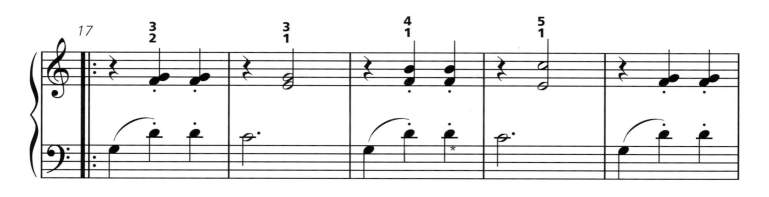

(2nd time al Fine)

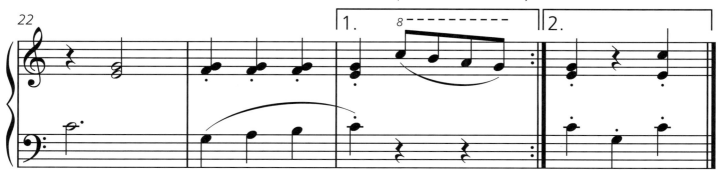

con moto = with movement, quickly

PLAYING CORNER

Practice need not always start from the beginning of a piece: you should try starting at a different place each time.

23

UNIT 3: Extending the Range of Notes in RH

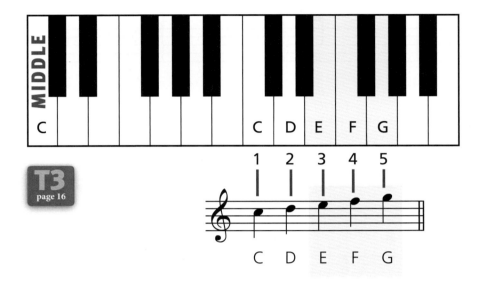

T3 page 16

Minuetto*

from *24 Short and Easy Pieces*, No.1

D3 page 12/13 **P3** page 14-16

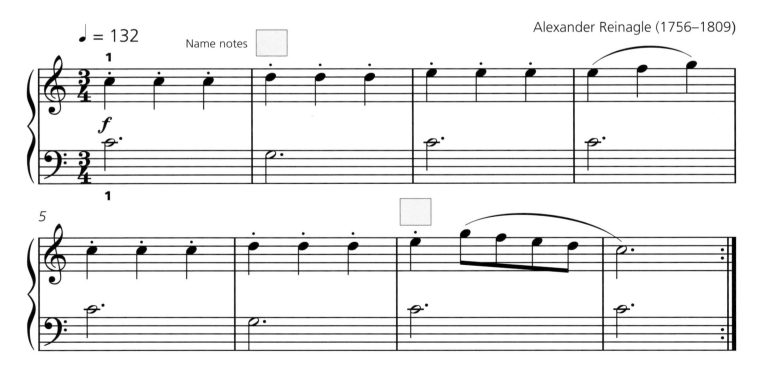

Alexander Reinagle (1756–1809)

♩ = 132   Name notes

© 2017 Schott Music Limited, London

*) **The Minuet** (Italian: Minuetto) was the most popular courtly dance in the 17th and 18th centuries. It is a partner dance in a moderately fast 3/4 time, characterized by small steps, intricate patterns and bows.

▶ Video **4** | Audio Track **16** | Rhythm Check **7** | Sight-Reading **8**

 Alexander Reinagle was an American pianist, piano teacher and composer of English origin. This Minuetto reflects his interest in teaching and his talent for composing simple and tuneful pieces for tuition purposes.

Sonatina

1st movement

Charles Henry Wilton (1761–1832)

Moderato ♩ = 144

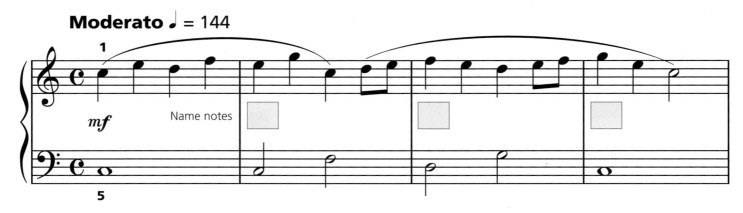

Name notes

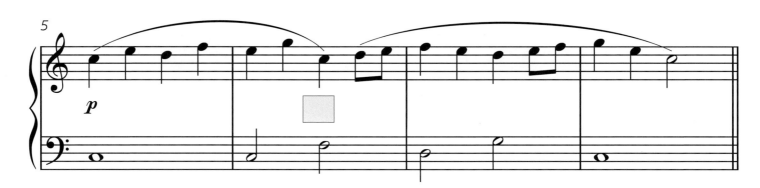

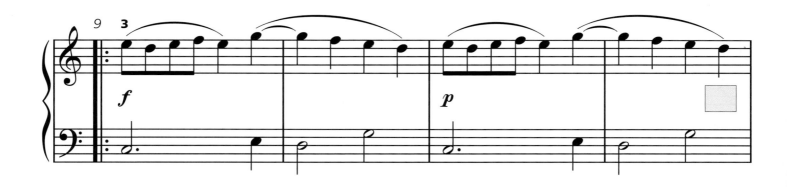

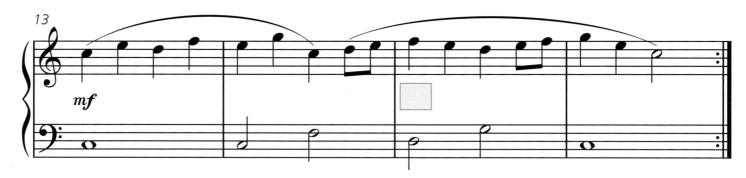

© 2017 Schott Music Limited, London

▶ Audio Track **17** | Rhythm Check **8**

 Charles Henry Wilton was an English violin and p ano teacher, violinist and composer.

Unit 4: Walking Fingers

B   B

Finger Fitness page 79, No. 15

 P3 page 19

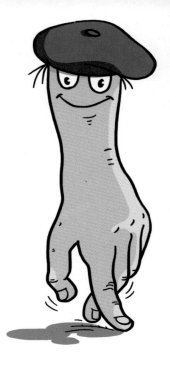

Exercise

HGH

♩. = 88

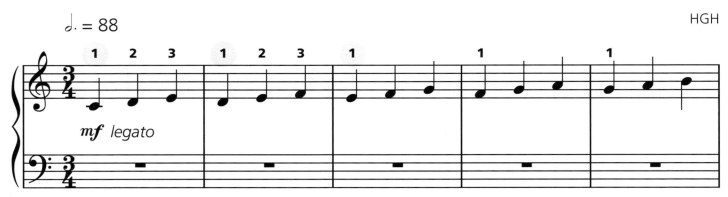

mf legato

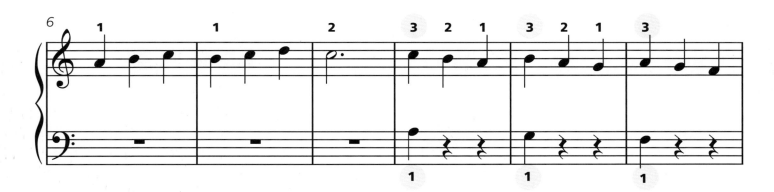

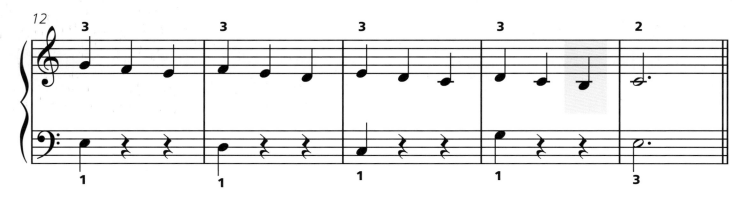

© 2017 Schott Music Limited, London

▶ Video **5** | Audio Track **18** | Rhythm Check **9** | Workout **4**

Autumn Leaves

 T3 page 18/19   P3 page 20

HGH

Andante ♩ = 88

© 2017 Schott Music Limited, London

espressivo, espr. = with expression

Sequence (Latin *sequi* = follow):
Repetition of a note pattern (motif),
starting on varying steps in the scale.

On this page there are two motifs with sequences.
Circle the bars/measures that contain sequences.

Unit 5: Interval of a Seventh

T3
page 20/21

On the piano

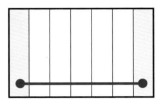

= distance of 7 notes

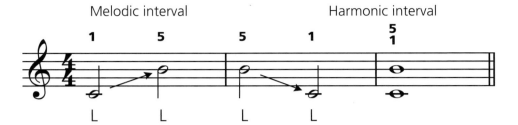

Melodic interval   Harmonic interval

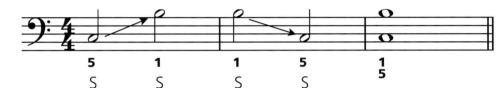

Melodic interval   Harmonic interval

D3
page 20-23

P3
page 21

Cool Junior Jazz

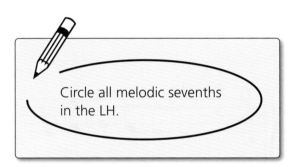

Circle all melodic sevenths in the LH.

Allegretto ♩ = 116

Intro

HGH

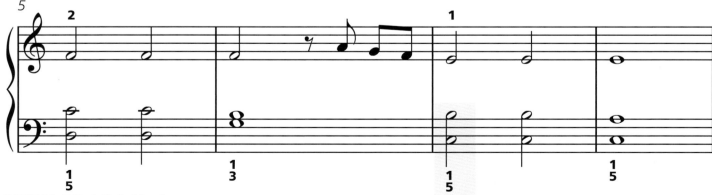

© 2017 Schott Music Limited, London

▶ Video **6** | Audio Track **20** | Workout **5** | Sight-Reading **10**

Name notes ☐ ☐   ☐ ☐

Unit 6: Interval of an Octave

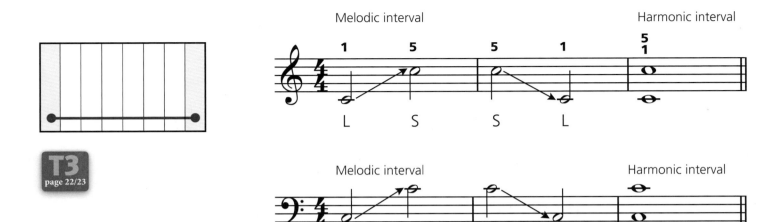

Melodic interval   Harmonic interval

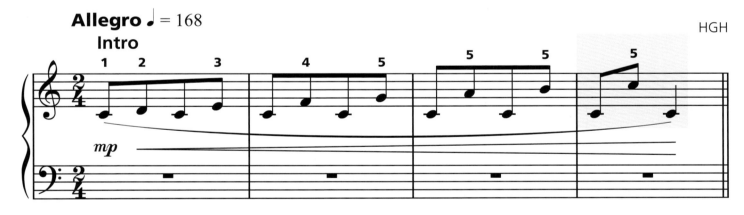

Melodic interval   Harmonic interval

Finger Fitness page 79, No. 16   **D3** page 24-27   **P3** page 22-24

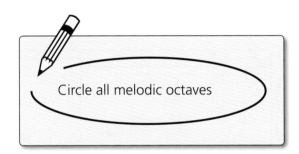

Circle all melodic octaves

Octave Polka*

Allegro ♩ = 168

HGH

Intro

mp

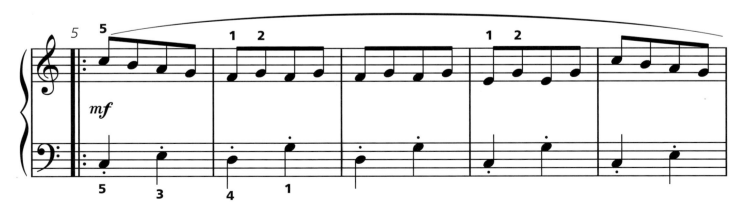

mf

© 2017 Schott Music Limited, London

▶ Video **7** | Audio Track **21** | Rhythm Check **11** | Workout **6** | Sight-Reading **11**

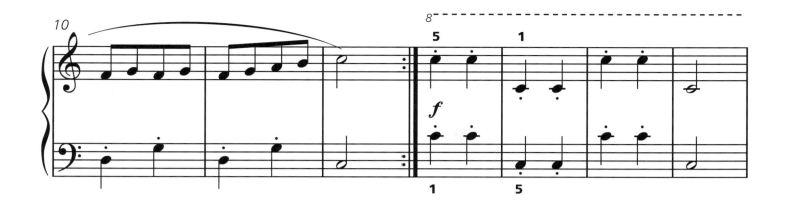

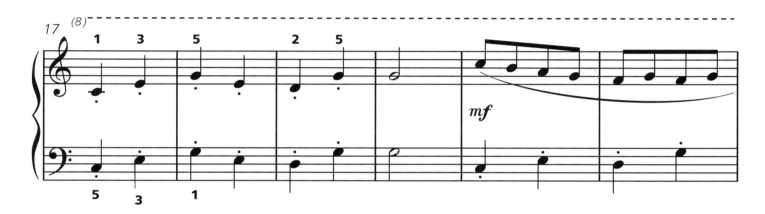

*) A **Polka** is a lively partner dance in 2/4 time that emerged in Bohemia (now the Czech Republic) in about 1830. Pairs of dancers stand in a large circle and dance in anti-clockwise direction.

Unit 7: Passing Under

T3
page 24/25

Another way of extending the five-note range, besides changing fingers on the same key and spreading the fingers, is passing thumb and fingers under and over each other. The thumb is of central importance here. It is important not to release the key until the next one is played.

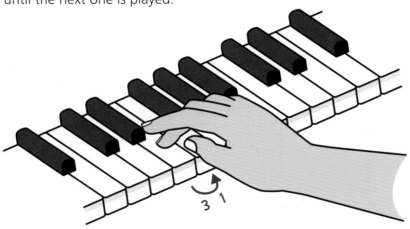

TECHNIQUE CORNER

When passing the thumb under the hand, move quickly – with the wrist relaxed and moved slightly to the side so the thumb can strike the next key comfortably. The other fingers then move to the new hand position without pressing down on keys, each finger resting on the relevant key for the duration of the dotted minim/half note.

Exercise

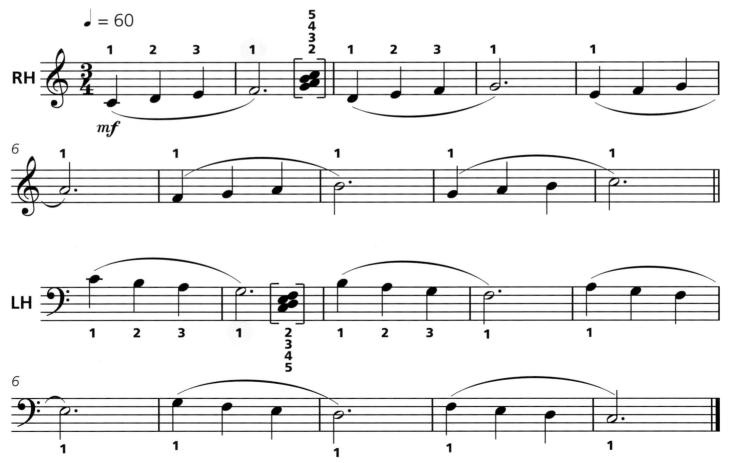

© 2017 Schott Music Limited, London

▶ Video **8** | Audio Track **22** | Workout **7**

Crossing Over

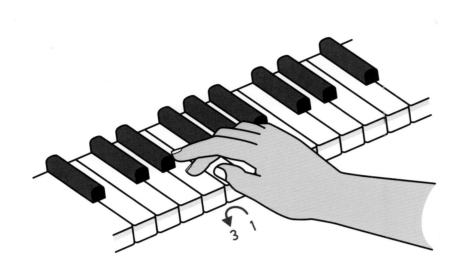

TECHNIQUE CORNER

When crossing over, the third finger moves over the thumb. The wrist moves slightly sideways and when the third finger has played the note, the thumb moves to the new position, remaining there for three beats.

Exercise

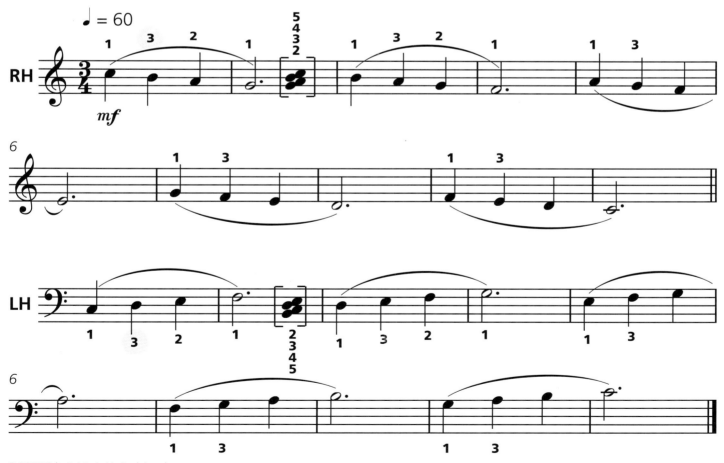

© 2017 Schott Music Limited, London

▶ Video **9** | Audio Track **23** | Workout **7**

Tightrope Dancer

Finger Fitness page 80, No. 17

HGH

Grazioso ♩ = 88

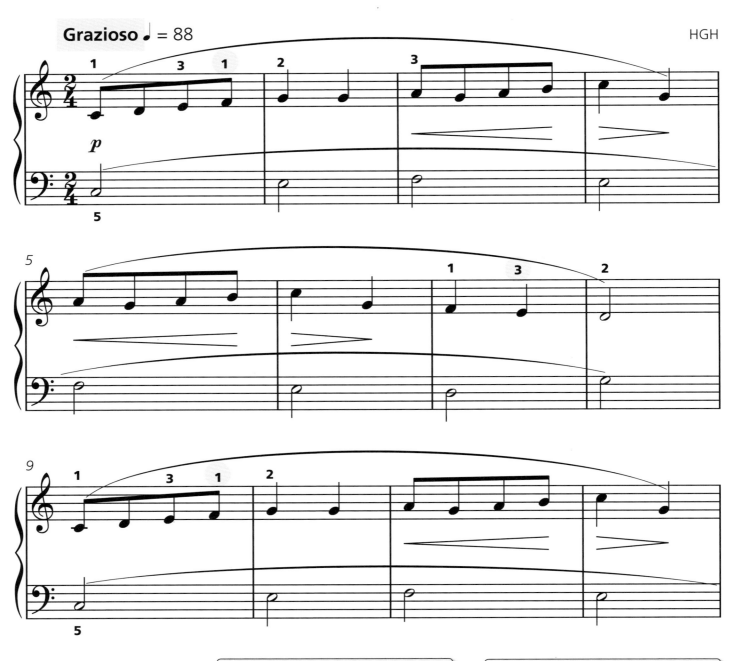

© 2017 Schott Music Limited, London

grazioso = graceful, charming

Opus, Op. = work, composition

▶ Audio Track **24** | Rhythm Check **12** | Sight-Reading **12**

Little Melodic Exercise

Finger Fitness page 80, No. 18

Op. 187, No. 30

♩ = 108

Cornelius Gurlitt (1820–1901)

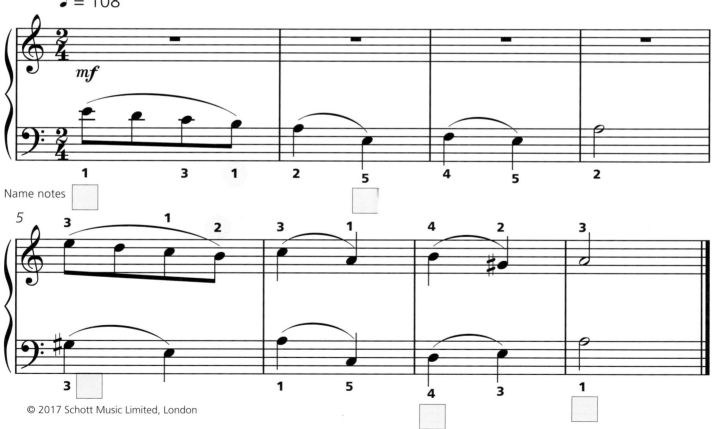

Name notes

© 2017 Schott Music Limited, London

Cornelius Gurlitt was a German piano teacher and composer, nowadays best known for his easy piano pieces for beginners.

My Bonnie Lies Over the Ocean

Finger Fitness | page 80, No. 19

Scottish Folk Song
Arr.: HGH

© 2017 Schott Music Limited, London

▶ Audio Track **26** | Rhythm Check **13**

Unit 8: Major Scales

The C Major Scale

The major scale consists of 8 notes. In music theory these scale degrees are indicated by **roman numerals:**
I II III IV V VI VII VIII

The scale begins and ends with the same note. The scale is named after this so-called keynote.

In the **major scale** there are **five whole tone steps/whole steps** and **two semi tone steps/half tone or half steps** between the notes. The **half tone steps occur between III & IV, and VII & VIII**. The seventh note leads back to the keynote and is therefore called the **leading note**.

The C major scale has no key signature. The major tonality is characterized by the **major third**, which is 4 half tone steps above the keynote. The major tonality is **bright, clear, and lively**.

The Construction of Major Scales

The C major scale

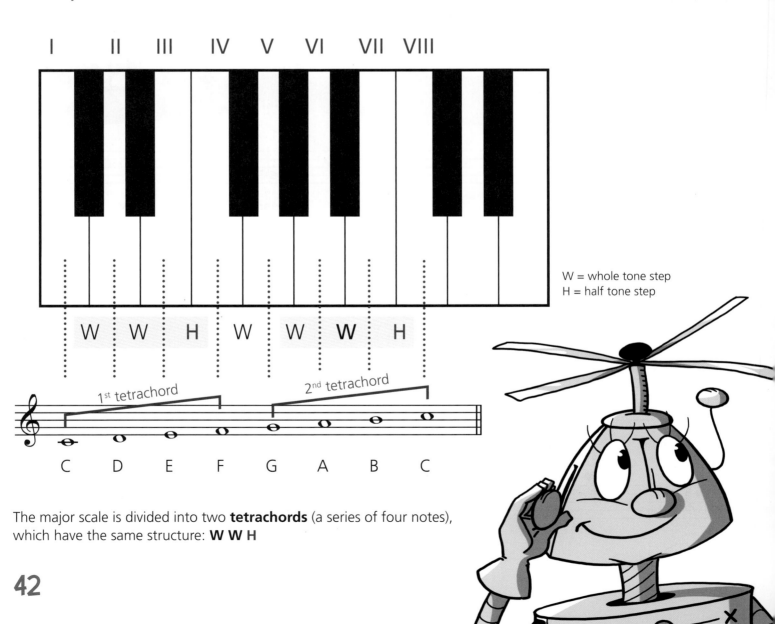

W = whole tone step
H = half tone step

The major scale is divided into two **tetrachords** (a series of four notes), which have the same structure: **W W H**

42

43

C Major Scale Exercises

1 Shared between both hands

2 RH alone

3 LH alone

4 RH and LH in contrary motion

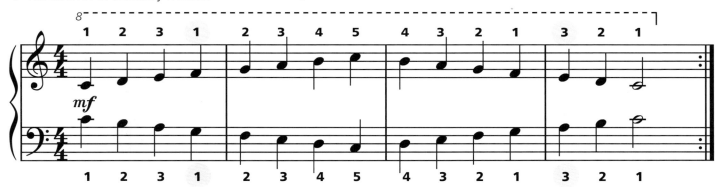

© 2017 Schott Music Limited, London

PLAYING CORNER

Fingering is very easy for the C major scale: play the eight notes with your five fingers as 5+3 or 3+5.

RH: upwards 3 (pass thumb under) + 5   downwards 5 (pass 3rd finger over) + 3
LH: upwards 5 (pass 3rd finger over) + 3   downwards 3 (pass thumb under) + 5

Flash Cards 3: Notes

The *Flash Cards* can be used to provide further practice in note reading, with musical symbols/terms and rhythm patterns. You can collect the cards from each book.

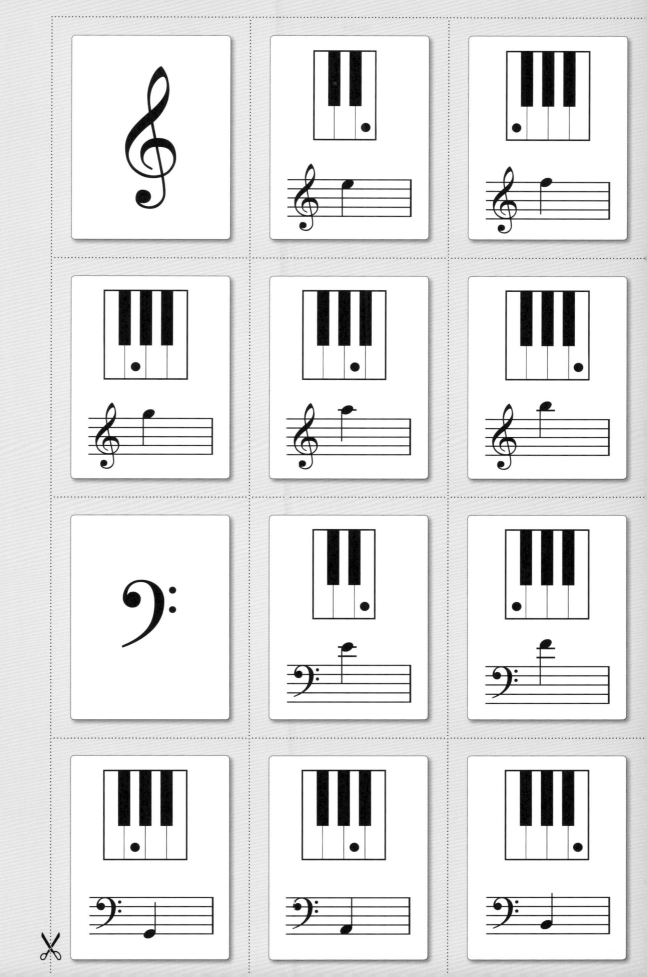

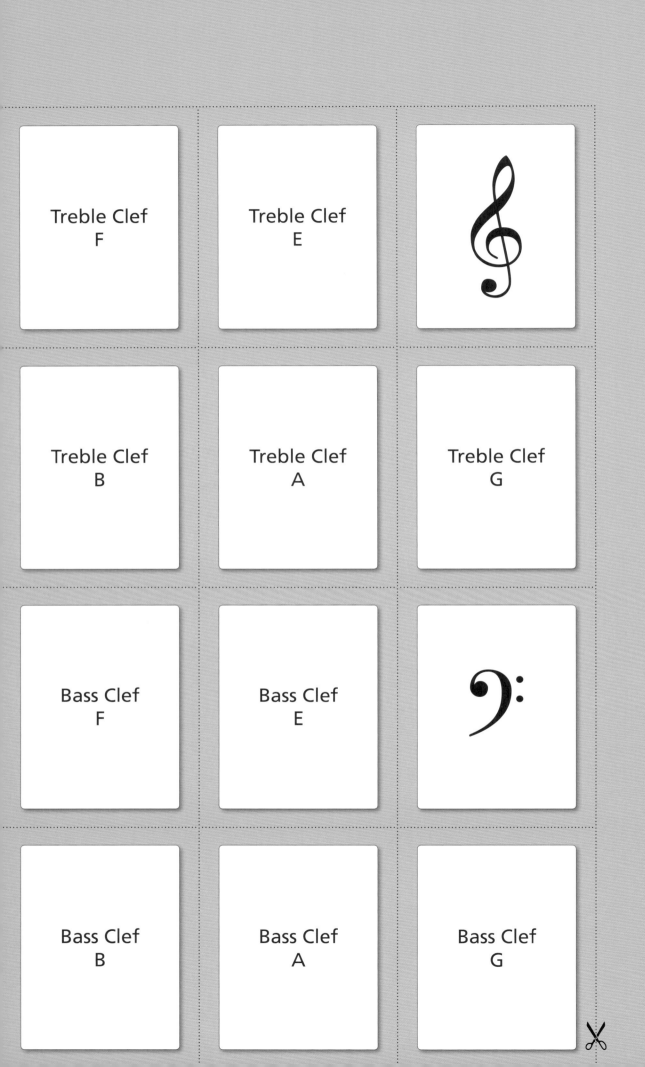

Treble Clef
F

Treble Clef
E

Treble Clef
B

Treble Clef
A

Treble Clef
G

Bass Clef
F

Bass Clef
E

Bass Clef
B

Bass Clef
A

Bass Clef
G

Flash Cards 3: Musical Symbols/Terms (1)

The *Flash Cards* can be used to provide further practice in note reading, with musical symbols/terms and rhythm patterns. You can collect the cards from each book.

Sequence	grazioso	C Major Triad/Chord	Step V (D) Chord in C Major
espr.	Interval of an Octave	C Major Scale	Step IV (S) Chord in C Major
Canon	Interval of a Seventh	non troppo	Step I (T) Chord in C Major
Metronome Markings	Interval of a Sixth	Op.	vivo

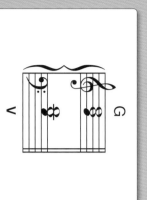

Dominant

V

G

Subdominant

IV

F

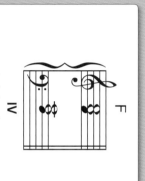

Tonic

I

C

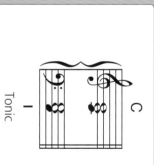

lively

C

Not too much

Opus
= work, composition

Graceful, charming

Distance of eight notes

Distance of seven notes

Distance of six notes

Repetition of a pattern of notes starting on various steps in the scale

espressivo
= with expression

A canon is a polyphonic piece for several voices where all voices play or sing the same tune, one after another.

A device that indicates the beat, helping to control the tempo of a piece.

Flash Cards 3: Musical Symbols/Terms (2)

The *Flash Cards* can be used to provide further practice in note reading, with musical symbols/terms and rhythm patterns. You can collect the cards from each book.

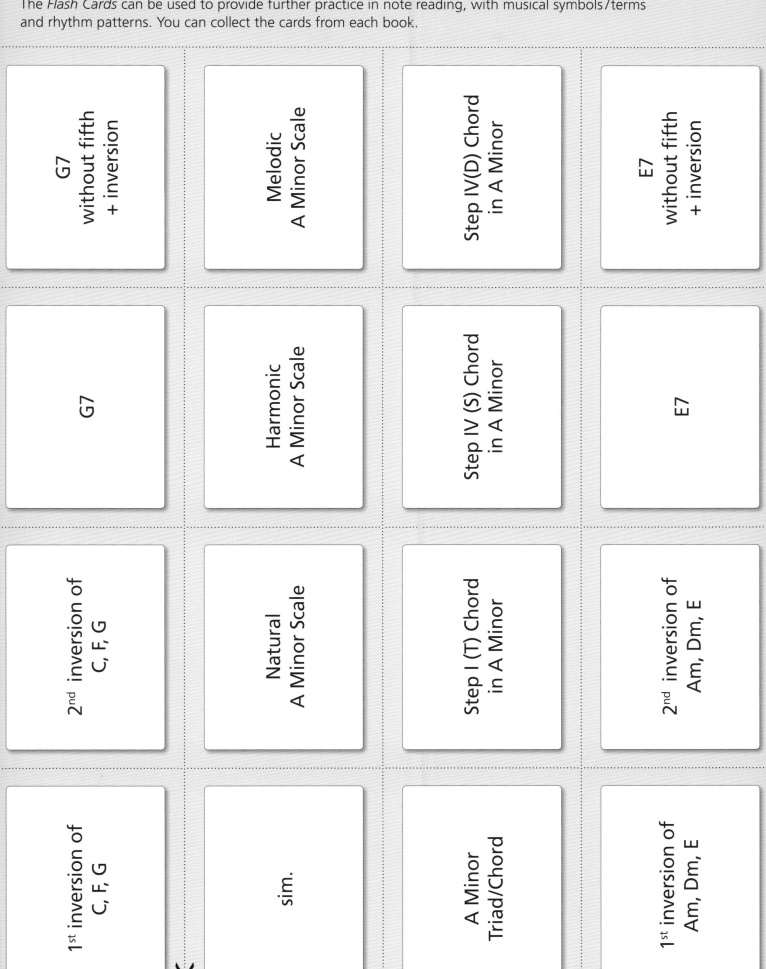

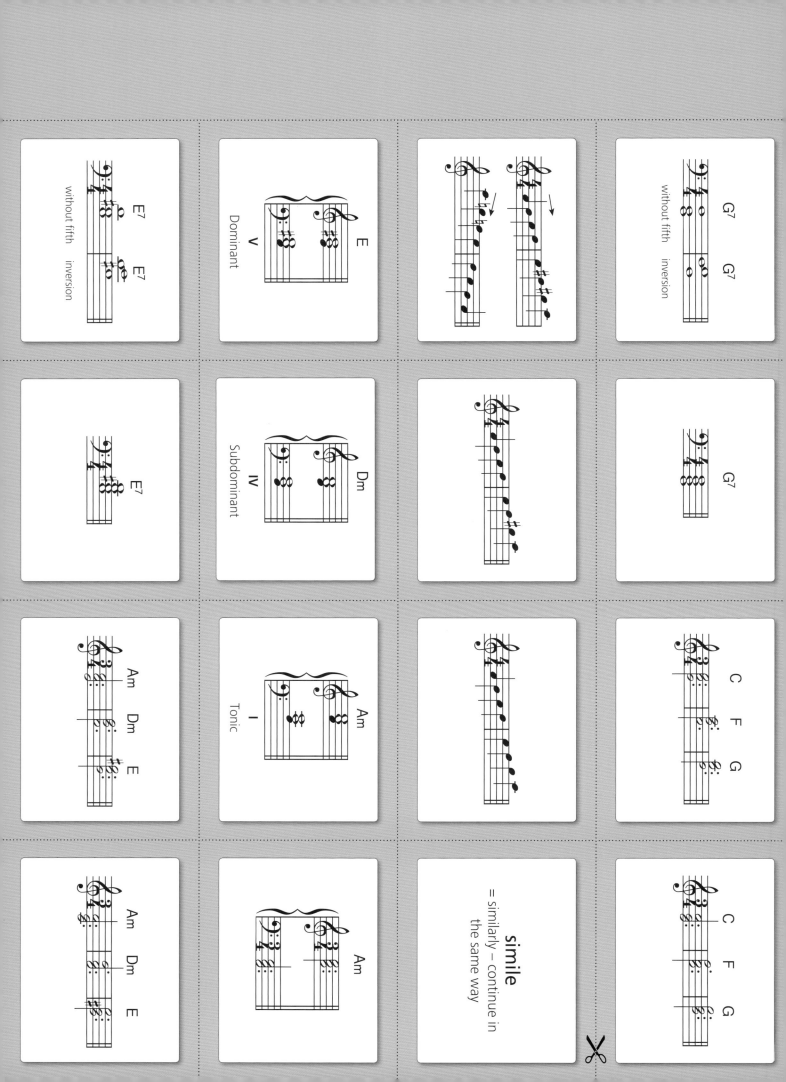

Flash Cards 3: Musical Symbols/Terms (3)

The *Flash Cards* can be used to provide further practice in note reading, with musical symbols/terms and rhythm patterns. You can collect the cards from each book.

Subdominant	Leading note	Minuet	Ostinato
Tonic	largo	Right Pedal	con moto
Coda	Dominant Seventh Chord	Minor Triad	*sf*
Chord	Dominant	Major Triad	Polka

Step IV of a major or minor scale

A note in a scale which leads back to the key note. In the major scale, for example, it is step VII.

The minuet was the most popular courtly dance in the 17th and 18th centuries. It is a partner dance in a moderately fast 3/4-time, characterized by small steps, intricate patterns and bows.

An Ostinato is a melodic or rhythmic figure, usually in the bass, which is constantly repeated; also known as *Basso Ostinato*.

Step I of a major or minor scale

Very slow, steady, stately. A Largo is a piece of music with a slow, steady tempo.

When you apply the pedal felt dampers are raised away from the strings, allowing them to vibrate freely, so notes sound for longer.

With movement, quickly

A coda is a concluding section added at the end of a composition.

A (four-note chord) on step V of the scale. From the root to the top note there is an interval of a seventh.

The minor triad consists of the 1st, 3rd and 5th notes of the minor scale.

sforzato
A very strong accent

A set of notes of different pitches sounded together.

Step V of a major or minor scale

The major triad consists of the 1st, 3rd and 5th notes of the major scale.

A polka is a lively partner dance in 2/4 time that emerged in Bohemia (now the Czech Republic) in about 1830. Pairs of dancers stand in a large circle and dance in anti-clockwise direction.

TECHNIQUE CORNER

➡ Play scales every day, ideally when starting practice, for they are very important.
➡ Play with separate hands at first, then hands together, starting slowly and then gradually increasing the tempo.

➡ Pay particular attention to passing the thumb under and crossing fingers over the thumb.
➡ Learn scales by heart.
➡ Try playing scales with a friend or your teacher playing along at a different octave pitch: it can be fun!

The Scale

Finger Fitness ➤ page 81, No. 20–21

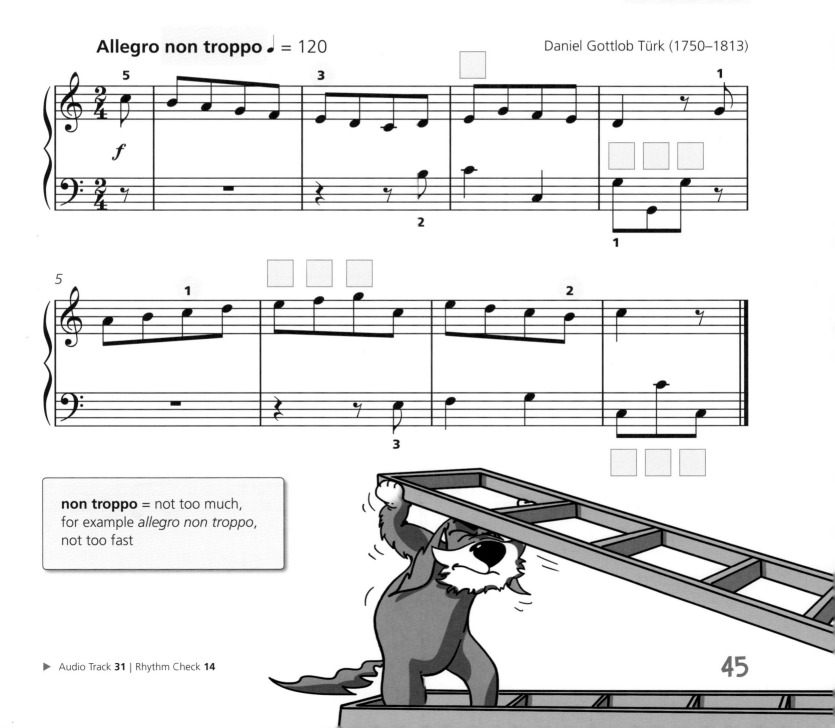

Allegro non troppo ♩ = 120

Daniel Gottlob Türk (1750–1813)

non troppo = not too much, for example *allegro non troppo*, not too fast

T3 page 30/31 **P3** page 32/33

Piano Halfpipe

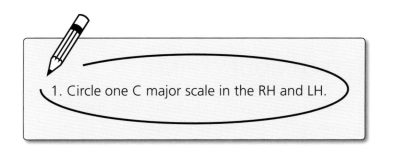

1. Circle one C major scale in the RH and LH.

♩ = 120

HGH

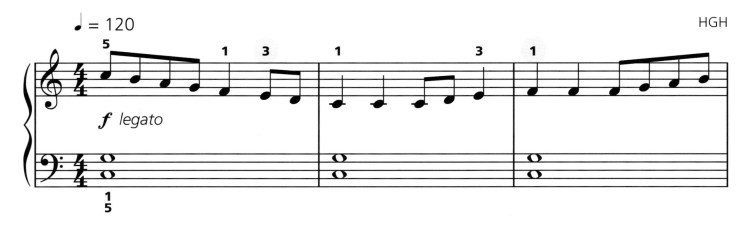

f legato

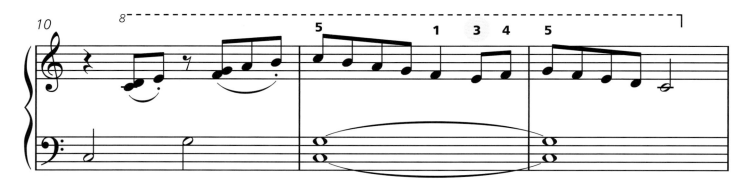

© 2017 Schott Music Limited, London

▶ Audio Track **32** | Rhythm Check **15** | Sight-Reading **13**

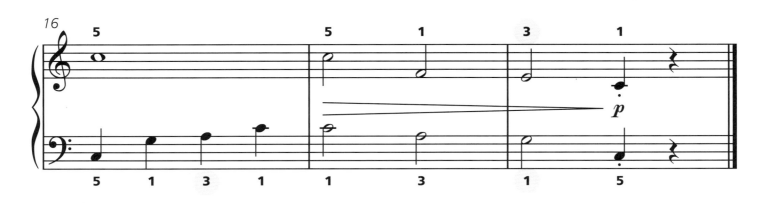

UNIT 9: Playing Triads

A **triad** consists of three notes: the **keynote**, **third** and **fifth**.
The **major triad** consists of the following notes from the **major scale**:

Keynote = 1st note

Third = 3rd note

Fifth = 5th note

The notes of the triad are either written on three lines or in three spaces.
The lowest note, the **keynote**, also gives the **name of the triad** or chord.
A **chord** is three or more notes of different pitch played at the same time.
A chord can have three, four, five notes or more.

The **chord symbol*** is determined by the keynote. **Chord symbol C stands for a C major triad.**

C Major Triad/Chord

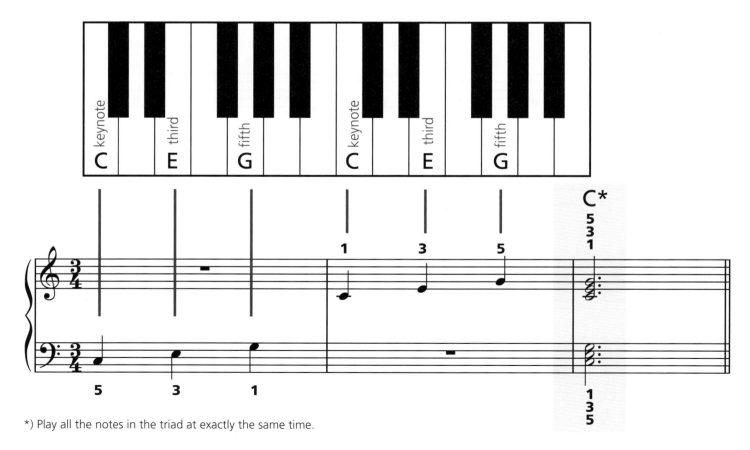

*) Play all the notes in the triad at exactly the same time.

48

C Major Triad Exercise

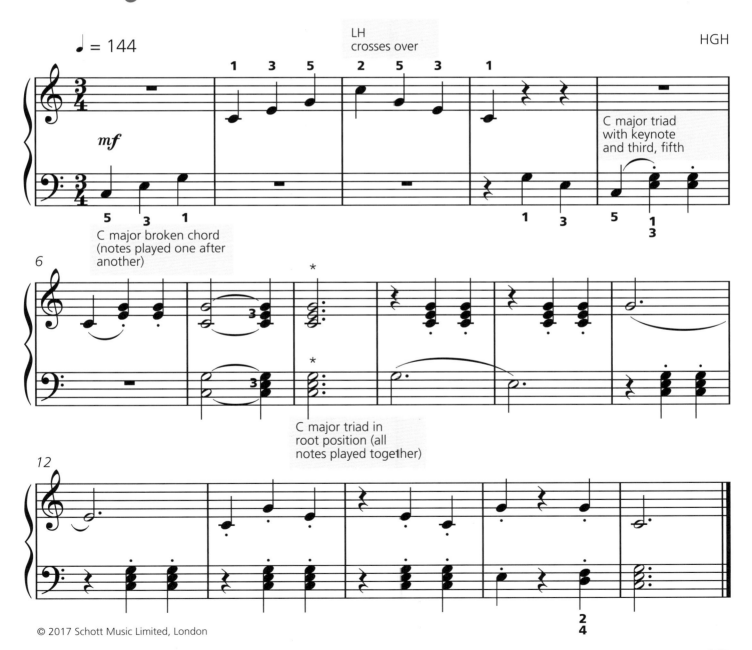

© 2017 Schott Music Limited, London

Unit 10: Primary Triads I IV V

➡ The chords on steps **I**, **IV** and **V** of the major scale are known as **primary triads**. The primary triads are also known as: **Step I = Tonic (T), Step IV = Subdominant (S), Step V = Dominant (D)**

Primary Triads in C Major

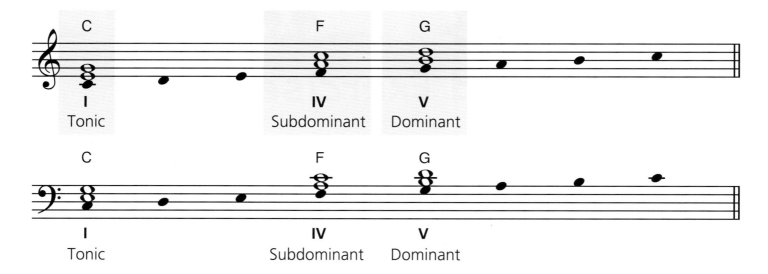

Primary Triads Exercise

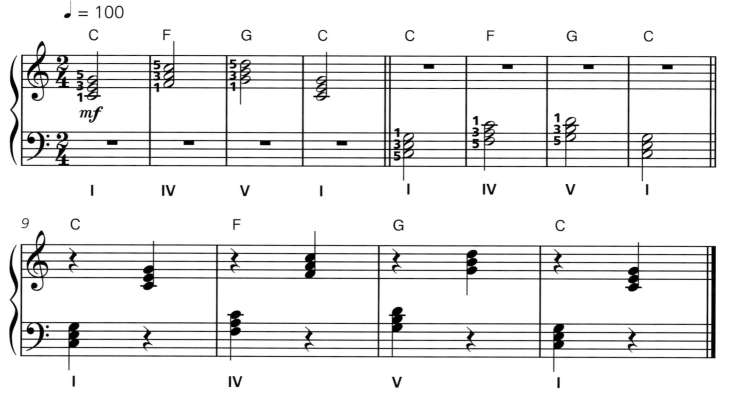

© 2017 Schott Music Limited, London

Hula Hoop

vivo = lively

Circle all IV chords.

Vivo ♩ = 126

Name notes ☐ ☐ ☐

HGH

© 2017 Schott Music Limited, London

Unit 11: Primary Triads and Inversions

➡️ An inversion is another arrangement of the notes of a triad.
➡️ Triads may be inverted by transposing the lowest note up an octave (**1st inversion**) or both the lower and middle notes up an octave (**2nd inversion**).

Primary Triads with Inversions in C Major

Play hands separately, starting with RH. LH plays an octave lower.

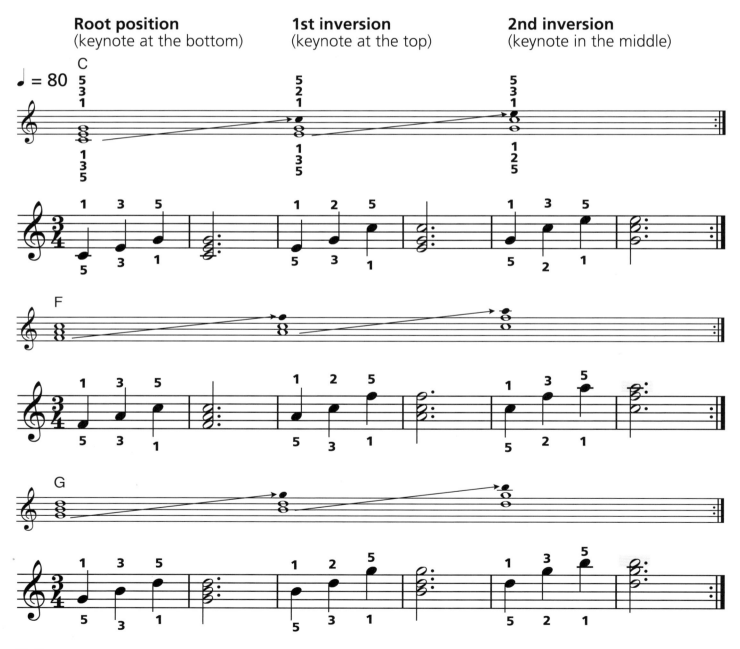

52

- ➡ Inversions can be used for smoother chord progressions that are easier to play.
- ➡ Using inversions means parts move as little as possible, with notes common to adjacent chords held on across chord changes.

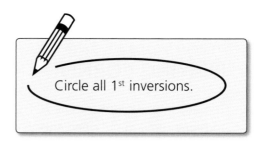

Circle all 1st inversions.

Aloha

HGH

Andante ♩ = 80

mf

C — Root position
F — 2nd inversion
G — 1st inversion
C — Root position

1

5 C 3
F 2
G 4

8 C 1
C 1
F 2
G

12 C
C 1 2 5
F 1 3
G *rit.*
C 1 2 4

1st inversion
Root position
2nd inversion
1st inversion

© 2017 Schott Music Limited, London

▶ Audio Track **37** | Rhythm Check **18** | Workout **10**

PLAYING CORNER

The accompaniment for ON TOP OF OLD SMOKY here only uses root position of chords.
To make moving between chords easier and to improve the sound you can use the following inversions for the F major and G major chord:

F major chord
(2nd inversion)

G major chord
(1st inversion)

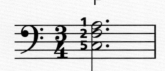

On Top of Old Smoky

American Folk Song
Arr.: HGH

© 2017 Schott Music Limited, London

▶ Audio Track **38/39**

PLAYING CORNER

Try playing ON TOP OF OLD SMOKY with this accompaniment, too.

On Top of Old Smoky

Variation

Circle all 2nd inversions.

American Folk Song
Arr.: HGH

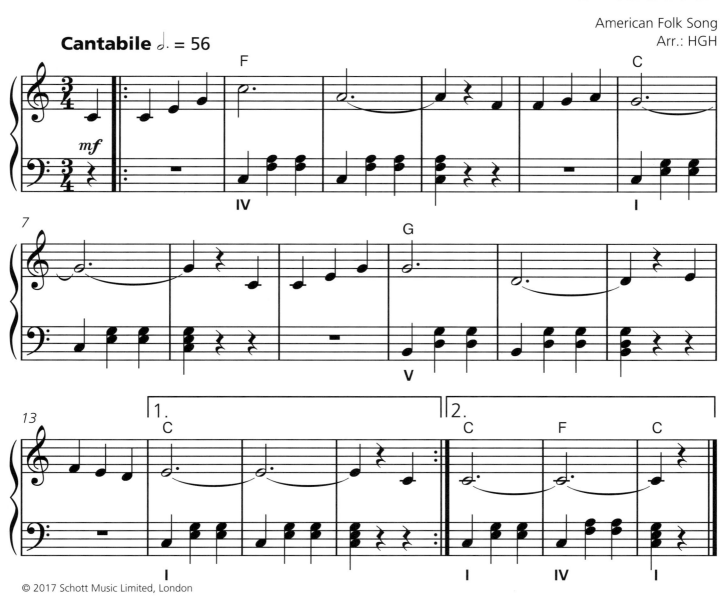

© 2017 Schott Music Limited, London

▶ Audio Track **40/41**| Workout **11**

55

UNIT 12:
Dominant Seventh Chord V7

➡ On step V, the dominant, three thirds are often layered on top of each other.

➡ From the root to the top note is an interval of a seventh.

➡ This chord is thus named the **dominant seventh chord**, abbreviated (in C major) to **G7**.

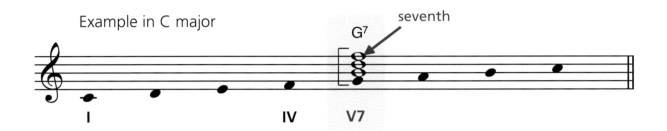

➡ If you want to play three notes rather than four, leave out the fifth.

➡ This chord often occurs in this inversion:

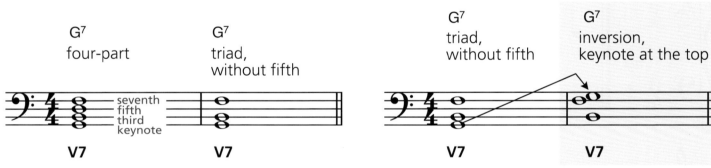

Preliminary Exercise

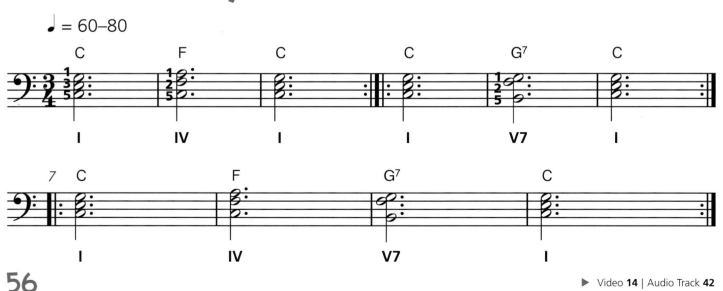

56

Down in the Lowlands

T3 page 32/33

♩ = 144

Friedrich Silcher (1789–1860)
Arr.: HGH

Circle broken V7 chords in the RH.

© 2017 Schott Music Limited, London

▶ Audio Track **43** | Rhythm Check **19** | Sight-Reading **15**

Cancan
from the operetta *Orpheus in the Underworld*

Presto ♩ = 132

Jacques Offenbach (1819–1880)
Arr.: HGH

© 2017 Schott Music Limited, London

Jacques Offenbach was a French composer of German origin. His most famous works are *Orpheus in the Underworld* (featuring the well-known *Cancan*) and *The Tales of Hoffmann*.

▶ Audio Track **44** | Rhythm Check **20** | Workout **12**

Try playing the CANCAN with these two accompaniments:

simile, sim. = similarly – continue in the same way

COMPOSING CORNER

You've already played TWINKLE, TWINKLE, LITTLE STAR – on page 11 in this Lesson Book. Now you can try accompanying that tune with chords you have learned. The example shows the first four bars/measures; play through the whole piece. It's quite easy!

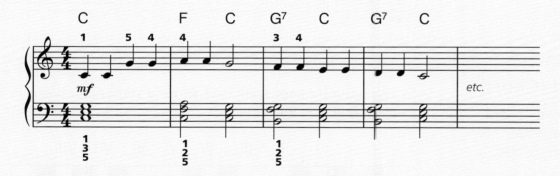

Try playing the piece with these two accompaniments:

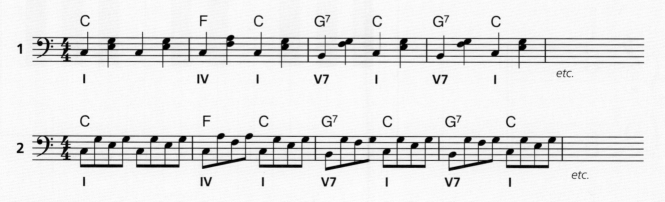

Alberti Bass
This use of a repeated broken chord pattern in the left hand is named after the composer and harpsichordist *Domenico Alberti* (c. 1710-1740) who used such figures extensively.

Unit 13: Minor Scales

A Minor Scales

Every major scale has a related, or relative minor scale sharing the same key signature.

Minor tonality is characterized by a **minor third** (= 3 half tone steps above the keynote).
If the keynote is A, the minor third is C. The minor third sounds dark, melancholy and sad.

The minor scale begins on step VI of the major scale.
There are three types of minor scales: **natural**, **harmonic** and **melodic**.

Natural A Minor Scale

The natural minor scale consists of the same notes as the relative major scale.

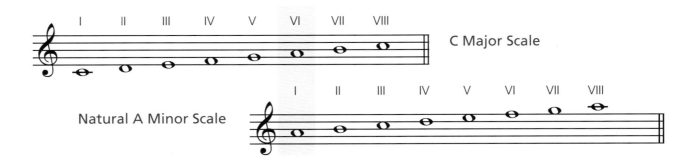

Natural A Minor Scale

A Minor Triad / Chord

The minor triad or minor chord consists of the 1st (keynote), 3rd (third) and 5th (fifth) notes of the minor scale.

Am

5
3
1

1
3
5

The chord symbol **Am** stands for the chord of A minor.

In the **natural minor scale** the **half tone steps** occur between steps **II & III**, and **V & VI**.

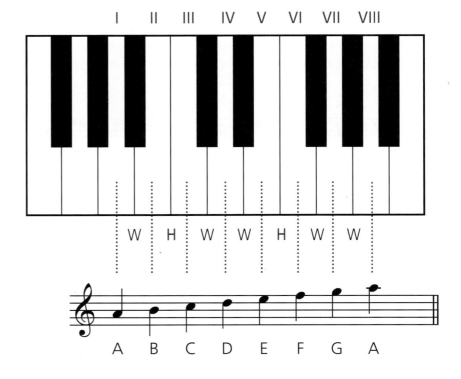

F   A

sforzato *sf*
= A very strong accent

Finger Fitness   page 81, No. 22-23

Whitewater Rafting

HGH

© 2017 Schott Music Limited, London
▶ Audio Track **47** | Rhythm Check **21**

Sad and Happy Amadeus

Andante ♩ = 80

HGH

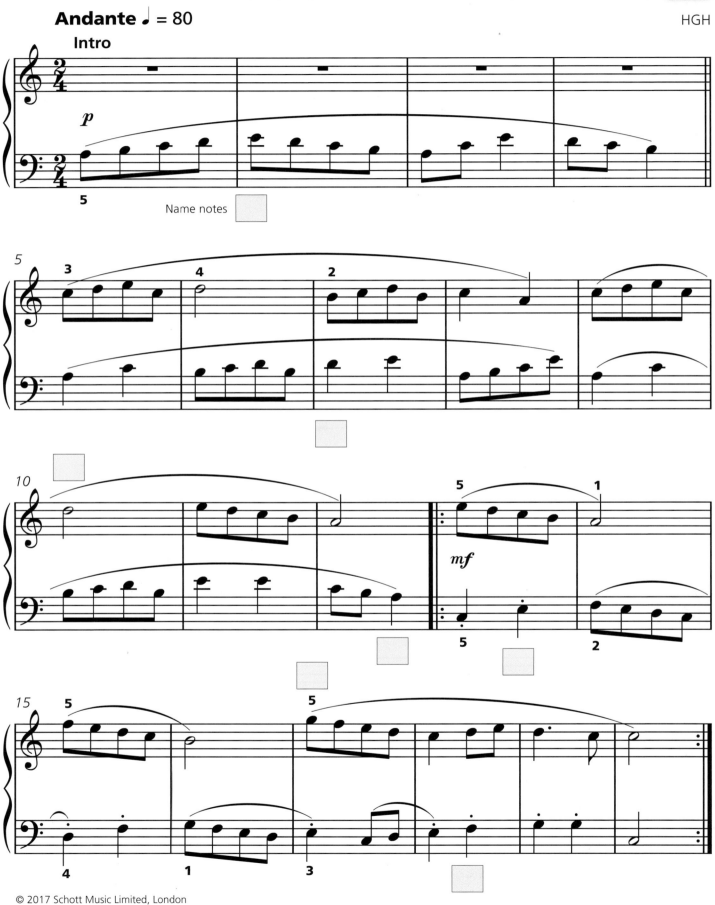

Name notes

© 2017 Schott Music Limited, London

▶ Audio Track **48** | Rhythm Check **22**

Harmonic A Minor Scale

The difference between the natural minor scale and the harmonic minor scale is that **step VII** in the harmonic scale **is raised by half a tone:** this must always be shown with an accidental preceding the note.
The harmonic minor scale is used more often than the natural scale, probably due to its raised seventh step – the leading note. This leads with a semitone / half step to the eighth note, the keynote, as in the major scale.
An unusual step of 3 semitones (1 ½ tones) now appears between steps VI and VII; this is a difficult interval to sing.

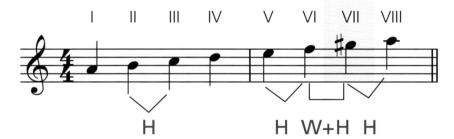

Melodic A Minor Scale

In this scale the interval of 1 ½ tones is avoided. If you wish to keep the half tone step between steps VII and VIII (the leading note), it is possible to **raise step VI by half a tone.**

In the melodic minor scale steps **VI and VII are thus raised by half a tone,** giving the second half of the scale a major character. They become **'natural' again when descending** and so the natural minor emerges.

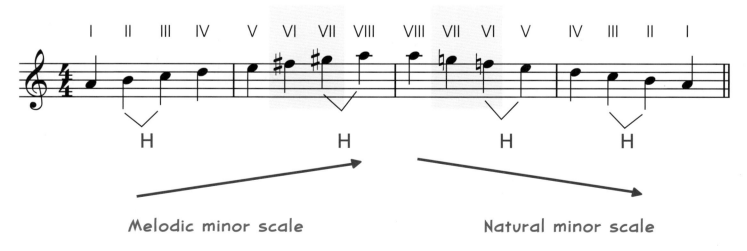

Melodic minor scale   Natural minor scale

▶ Video **15**

Flying Carpet

Finger Fitness page 82, No. 24–25

HGH

© 2017 Schott Music Limited, London

Unit 14: Primary Triads I IV V7
Primary Triads in A Minor

➡ The following chords on step V are based on the harmonic minor scale as this is the most commonly used form.

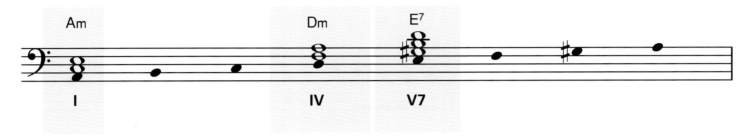

Primary Triads with Inversions in A Minor

Play hands separately, starting with LH.
RH plays an octave higher in the repeat.

Preliminary Exercise

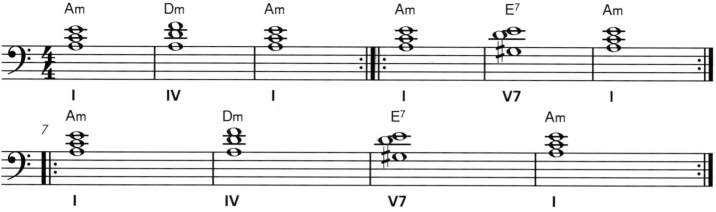

Bella ciao

Finger Fitness page 82, No. 26-27

D3 page 32-37 **P3** page 39

Italian Folk Song
Arr.: HGH

U - na mat - ti - na__ mi son sveg - lia - to,__ o bel - la, ciao, bel - la ciao, bel - la

ciao, ciao, ciao! U - na mat - ti - na__ mi son sveg - lia - to,__ e ho tro-

-va - to l'in - va - sor. U - na ma - sor.

© 2017 Schott Music Limited, London ▶ Audio Track **51/52** | Rhythm Check **24** | Workout **13** | Sight-Reading **16**

Unit 15: The Right Pedal (Sustaining Pedal)

The **right pedal**, also known as the **sustaining pedal**, is used to sustain and connect notes. When you apply the pedal felt dampers are raised away from the strings, allowing them to vibrate freely, so notes sound for longer.

The sustaining pedal is used with the right foot. The heel remains firmly on the ground and the ball of the foot remains in contact with the pedal.

The pedalling symbol is a bracket, which shows you exactly how and when to use the pedal. The pedal is normally applied after keys are played.

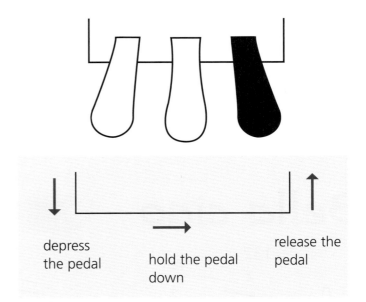

depress the pedal   hold the pedal down   release the pedal

Pedal Exercise 1

Process:
- Play the note C
- After playing the note – on beat 2 – depress the pedal
- Hold the pedal down
- As you play the next note, raise the pedal
- Then immediately press the pedal down again
- etc. (simile)

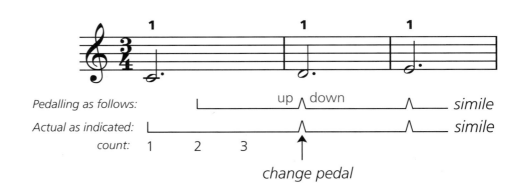

Pedalling as follows:

Actual as indicated:

count: 1   2   3

change pedal

Pedal Exercise 2

- Repeat the exercise above playing chords with the RH

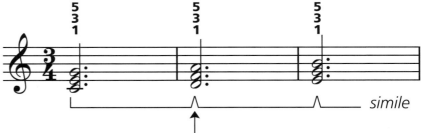

change pedal

▶ Video **17** |
Workout **14**

Moonlight

T3 page 42/43

HGH

♩. = 66

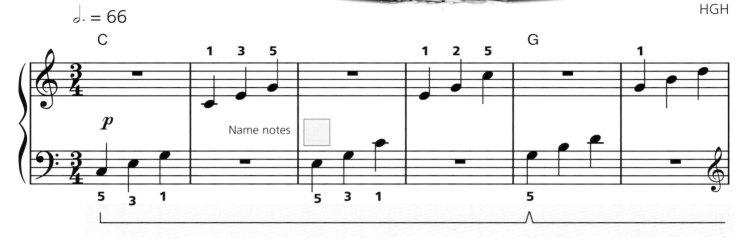

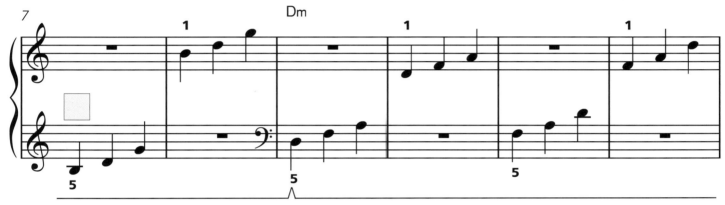

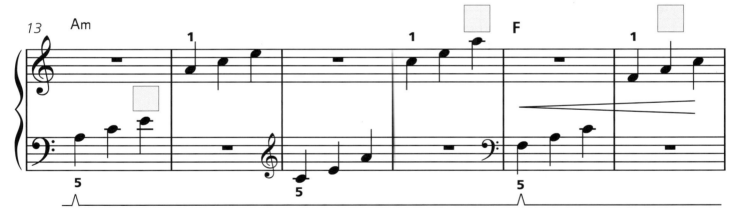

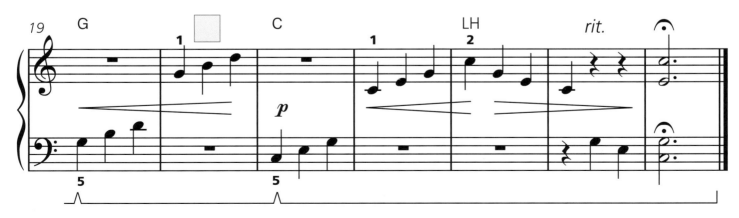

© 2017 Schott Music Limited, London

▶ Audio Track **53** | Workout **14** | Sight-Reading **17**

What Shall We Do with the Drunken Sailor

Sea Shanty from Ireland
Arr.: HGH

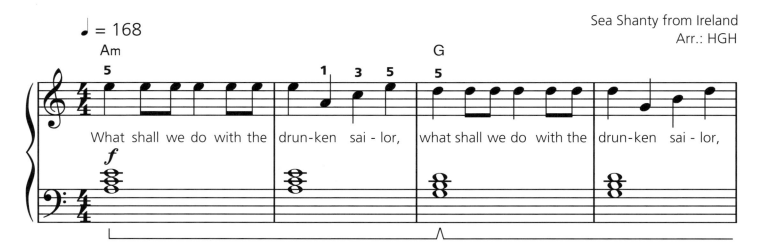

What shall we do with the drun-ken sai-lor, what shall we do with the drun-ken sai-lor,

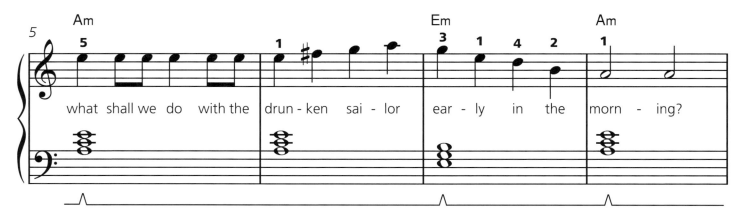

what shall we do with the drun-ken sai-lor ear-ly in the morn-ing?

© 2017 Schott Music Limited, London

▶ Audio Track **54** | Rhythm Check **25**

Try playing WHAT SHALL
WE DO WITH THE
DRUNKEN SAILOR
with these two
accompaniments:

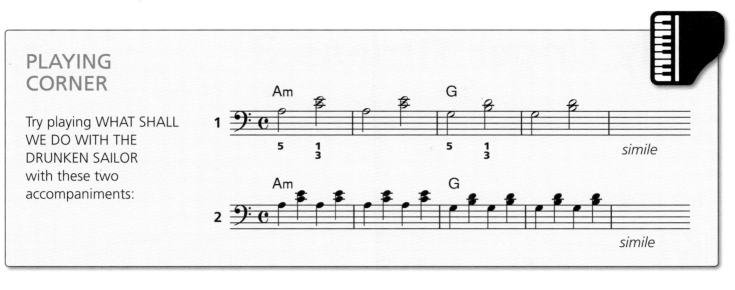

Hoo - ray, and up she ri - ses, hoo - ray, and up she ri - ses,

hoo - ray, and up she ri - ses ear - ly in the morn - ing.

▶ Audio Track **55/56**

Daily Finger Fitness 3

Progressively graded daily elementary finger exercises for developing finger strength and independence, evenness, accuracy and speed playing, as well as articulation and general musicality

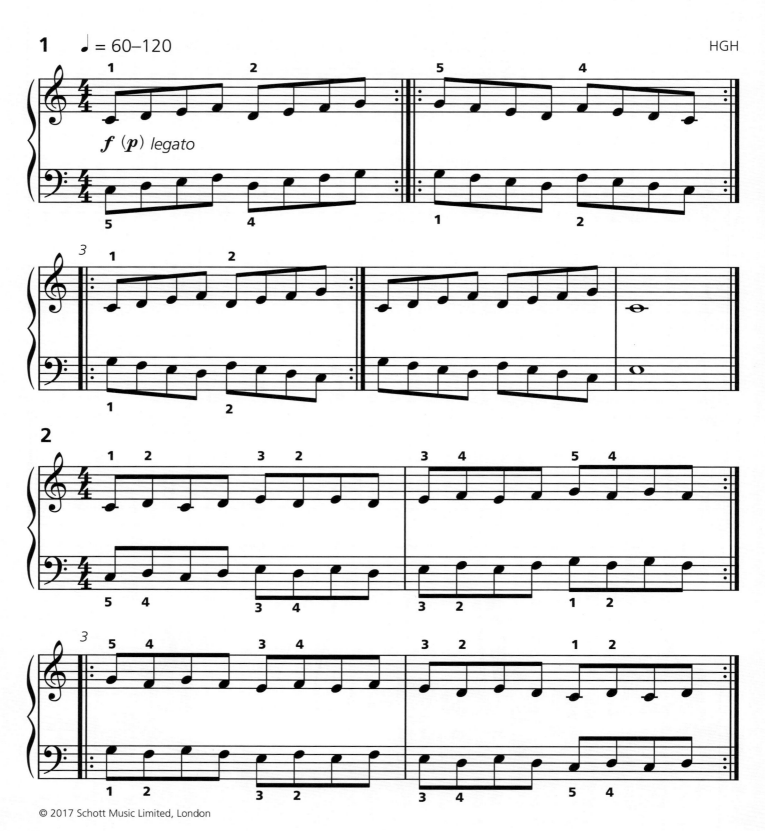

1 ♩ = 60–120

HGH

f (*p*) legato

2

© 2017 Schott Music Limited, London

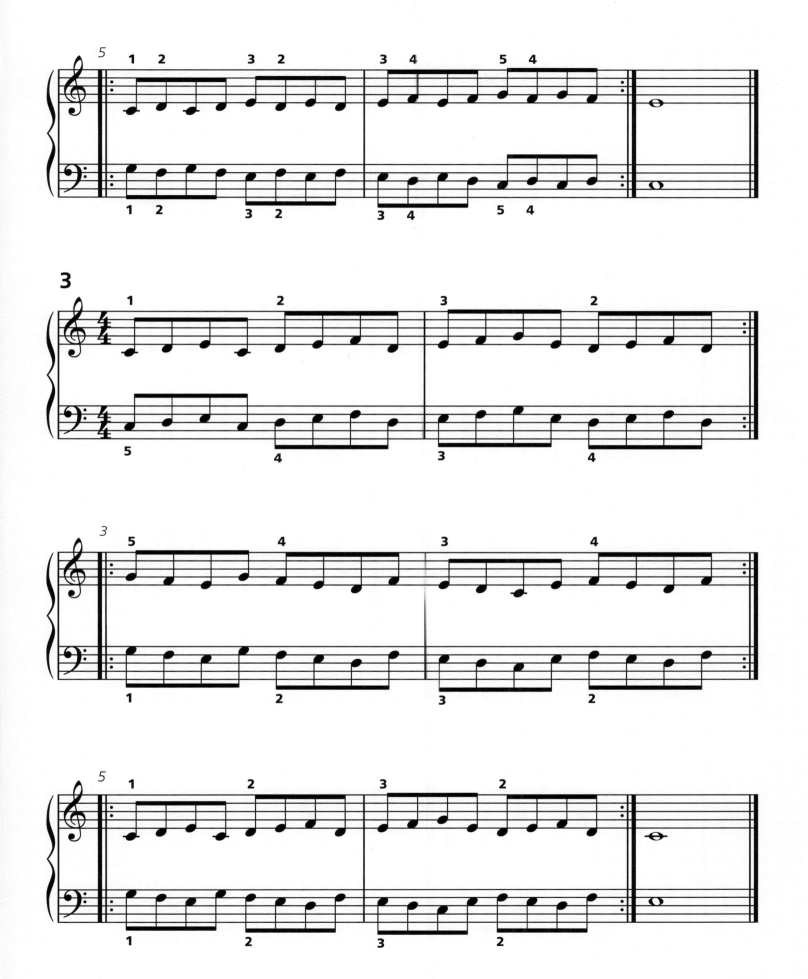

3

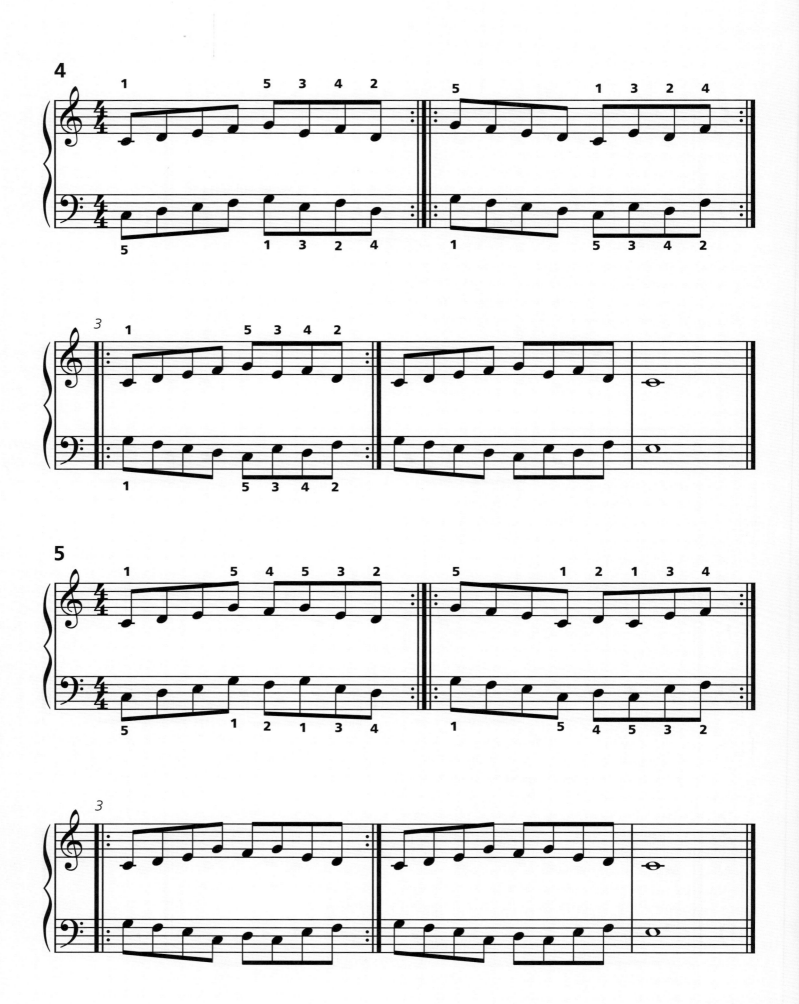

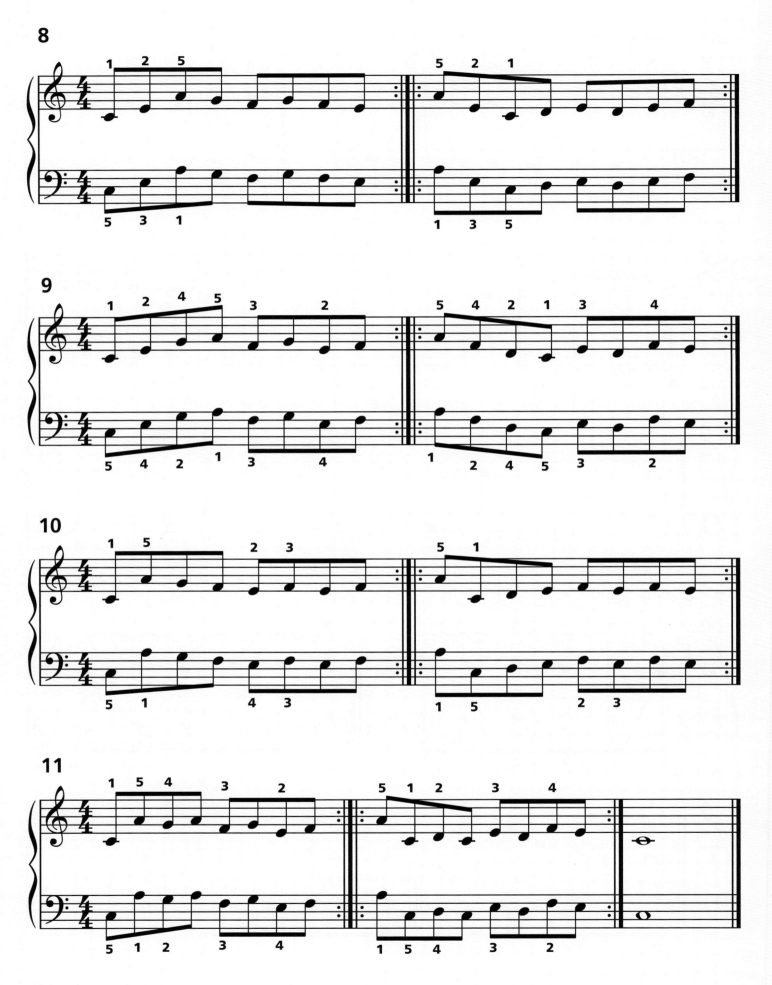

12

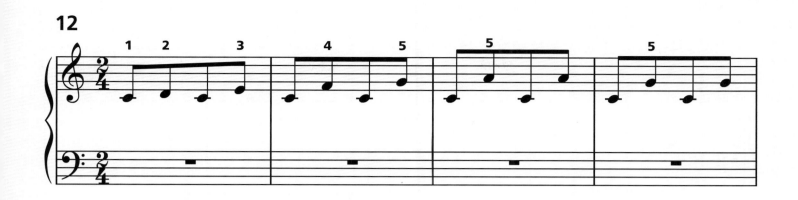

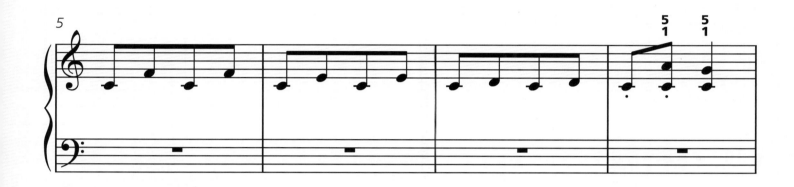

17

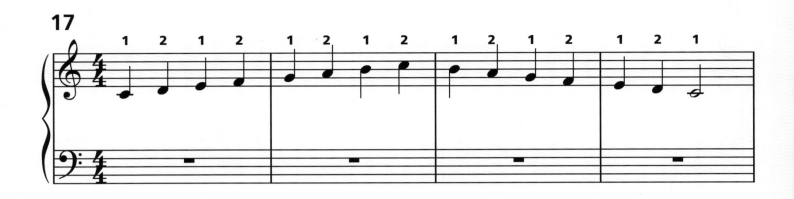

18

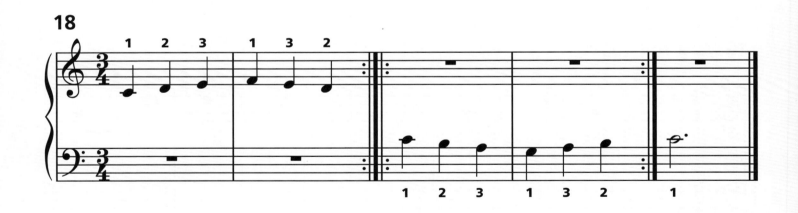

19   ♩ = 60–120

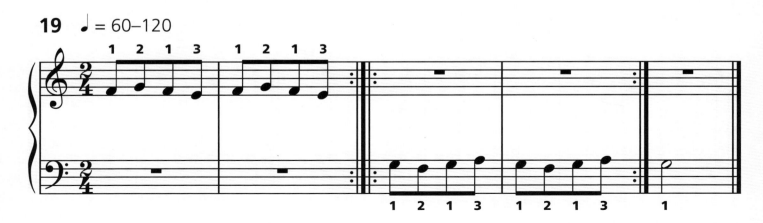

 = 100–200

20 **C Major** (Parallel Motion)

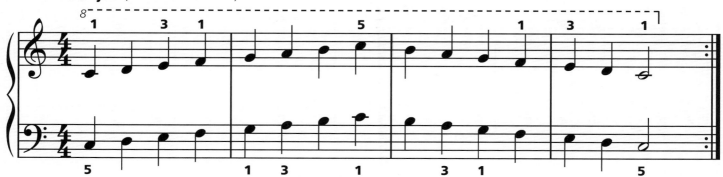

21 **C Major** (Contrary Motion)

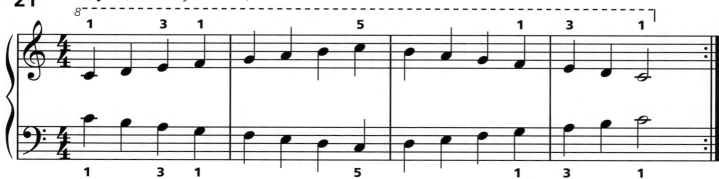

22 **Natural A Minor** (Parallel Motion)

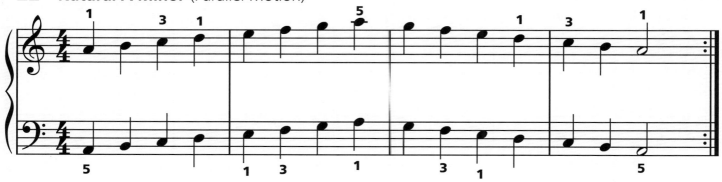

23 **Natural A Minor** (Contrary Motion)

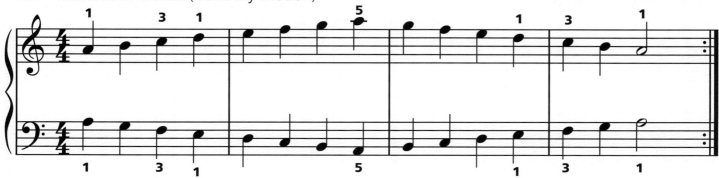

24 **Harmonic A Minor** (Parallel Motion)

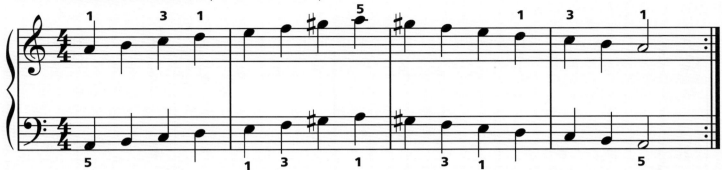

25 **Harmonic A Minor** (Contrary Motion)

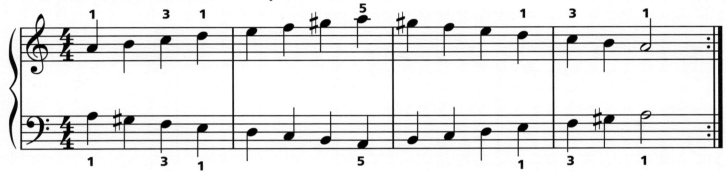

26 **Melodic A Minor** (Parallel Motion)

27 **Melodic A Minor** (Contrary Motion)

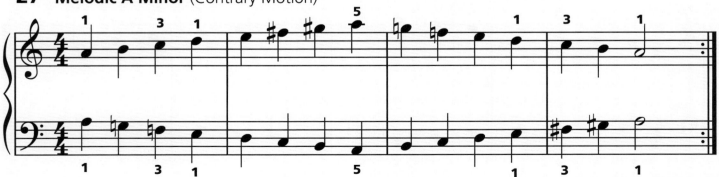

F Major 5-Note Pattern   F   F Minor 5-Note Pattern

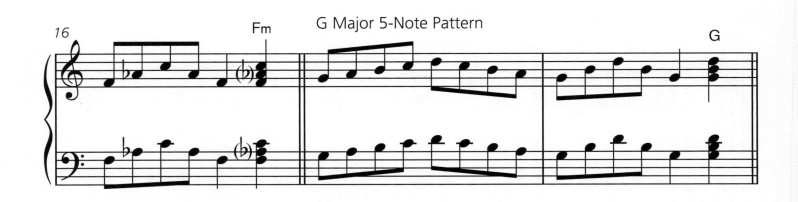

Fm   G Major 5-Note Pattern   G

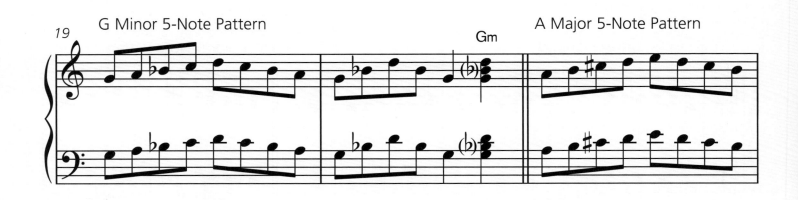

G Minor 5-Note Pattern   Gm   A Major 5-Note Pattern

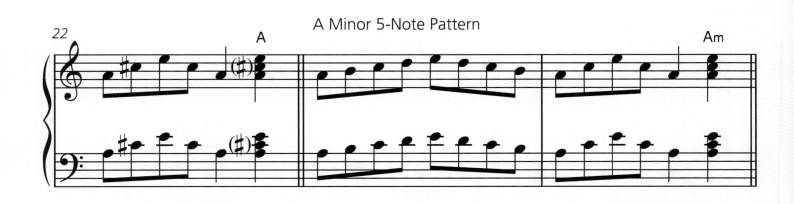

A Minor 5-Note Pattern   A   Am

B Major 5-Note Pattern

B Minor 5-Note Pattern

C Major 5-Note Pattern

C Minor 5-Note Pattern

Important Words and Signs

	Alberti bass	A musical figure consisting of similar repeated broken chords in the left hand. Named after *Domenico Alberti* (c. 1710-1740).
	Boogie-Woogie	Boogie-Woogie is a blues piano style that emerged in about 1920 among African-Americans in Chicago. Typical of the boogie (-woogie) is a rigid bass pattern that stays the same all the time beneath a rhythmically varied melody.
	Canon	A canon is a polyphonic piece for several voices where all voices play or sing the same tune, one after another.
	Chord	A set of notes of different pitches sounded together.
	Coda	A coda is a concluding section added at the end of a composition.
	con moto	With movement, quickly
V	Dominant (D)	Step V of a major or minor scale
V7	Dominant seventh chord (D7)........	A four-note chord on step V of the scale. From the root to the top note there is an interval of a seventh.
	Drone................................	A Drone is the term for one or two accompanying or held notes, played as the accompaniment to a melody. The bagpipes are typical drone instruments. The drone is the most simple form of polyphony.
espr.	espressivo	With expression
	grazioso	Graceful, charming
	Inversion	Chords do not only appear in root position (with the keynote, or tonic, at the bottom), but also in so-called inversions. These are created by transposing the lowest note up an octave (1st inversion), or both the lower and the middle notes up an octave (2nd inversion).
	largo	Very slow, steady, stately; A Largo is a piece of music with a slow, steady tempo.
	Leading note	A note in a scale which leads back to the keynote. In the major scale, for example, it is step VII.
	Major scale..........................	The major scale consists of eight notes or steps. Semitone steps/half steps occur between steps III & IV and steps VII & VIII.

	Major triad	The major triad consists of the 1ˢᵗ, 3ʳᵈ and 5ᵗʰ notes of the major scale.
	Metronome markings	A device that indicates the beat, helping to control the tempo of a piece.
	Minor scale..	The minor scale begins on step VI of the major scale to which it is related, and has the same key signature.
	Minor triad	The minor triad consists of the 1ˢᵗ, 3ʳᵈ and 5ᵗʰ notes of the minor scale.
	Minuet	The Minuet was the most popular courtly dance in the 17ᵗʰ and 18ᵗʰ centuries. It is a partner dance in a moderately fast 3/4 time, characterized by small steps, intricate patterns and bows.
	non troppo	Not too much
	Octave	Distance of eight notes
Op.	Opus	Work, composition
	Ostinato	An Ostinato is a melodic or rhythmic figure, usually in the bass, which is constantly repeated; also known as *Basso Ostinato*.
	Polka	A Polka is a lively partner dance in 2/4 time that emerged in Bohemia (now the Czech Republic) in about 1830. Pairs of dancers stand in a large circle and dance in anti-clockwise direction.
I IV V	Primary triads	Triads constructed on steps I, IV and V of the major or minor scales
⌊_____⌋	Right Pedal	When you apply the pedal felt dampers are raised away from the strings, allowing them to vibrate freely, so notes sound for longer.
	Seventh	Distance of seven notes
	Sequence	Repetition of a note pattern (motif) starting on varying steps in the scale.
sf	sforzato	A very strong accent
sim.	simile	Similarly – continue in the same way
	Sixth	Distance of six notes
S	Subdominant	Step IV of a major or minor scale
T	Tonic	Step I of a major or minor scale
	vivo	Lively

Certificate of Merit

Student _____

has successfully completed

Book 3 of the PIANO JUNIOR method

Teacher _____

Date _____

My favourite piece was _____